SCHOLASTIC

100
DESIGN & TECHNOLOGY LESSONS

Terms and conditions

IMPORTANT – PERMITTED USE AND WARNINGS – READ CAREFULLY BEFORE USING

IF YOU ACCEPT THE ABOVE CONDITIONS YOU MAY PROCEED TO USE THE CD-ROM.

Recommended system requirements:

- Windows: XP (Service Pack 3), Vista (Service Pack 2) or Windows 7 with 2.33GHz processor
- Mac: OS 10.6 to 10.8 with Intel Core™ Duo processor
- 1GB RAM (recommended)
- 1024 x 768 Screen resolution
- CD-ROM drive (24x speed recommended)
- 16-bit sound card
- Microsoft Word

For all technical support queries, please phone Scholastic Customer Services on 0845 6039091.

SCHOLASTIC

Book End, Range Road, Witney, Oxfordshire, OX29 0YD

www.scholastic.co.uk

© 2014, Scholastic Ltd

1 2 3 4 5 6 7 8 9   4 5 6 7 8 9 0 1 2 3

British Library Cataloguing-in-Publication Data
A catalogue record for this book is available from the
British Library.

ISBN 978-1407-14085-8
Printed by Bell & Bain Ltd, Glasgow

Authors
Laurence Keel and Julia Stanton

Editorial
Robin Hunt, Lucy Tritton and Sara Wiegand

Cover Design
Nicolle Thomas

Design Team
Nicolle Thomas and Black Dog Design

Illustrations
Moreno Chiacchiera (Beehive illustration)

Contents

Introduction	4

Year 1

Long-term planning	6
Overview of progression	7
Medium-term planning	8
Background knowledge	14

Year 2

Long-term planning	15
Overview of progression	16
Medium-term planning	17
Background knowledge	23

Year 3

Long-term planning	24
Overview of progression	25
Medium-term planning	26
Background knowledge	32

Year 4

Long-term planning	33
Overview of progression	34
Medium-term planning	35
Background knowledge	41

Year 5

Long-term planning	42
Overview of progression	43
Medium-term planning	44
Background knowledge	50

Year 6

Long-term planning	51
Overview of progression	52
Medium-term planning	53
Background knowledge	59
Progression across the key stages	60

Introduction

Design and technology is an inspiring, rigorous and practical subject. Using creativity and imagination, children design and make products that solve real and relevant problems within a variety of contexts, considering their own and others' needs, wants and values. They acquire a broad range of subject knowledge and draw on disciplines such as, mathematics, science, engineering, computing and art. Children learn how to take risks, becoming resourceful, innovative, enterprising and capable citizens. Through the evaluation of past and present design and technology, they develop a critical understanding of its impact on daily life and the wider world. High quality design and technology education makes an essential contribution to the creativity, culture, wealth and well-being of the nation. (*Purpose of study, National Curriculum in England: Design and Technology, 2013*)

The 2014 National Curriculum explains the purpose and aims, as follows:

> *The National Curriculum for design and technology aims to ensure that all children:*
> - *develop the creative, technical and practical expertise needed to perform everyday tasks confidently and to participate successfully in an increasingly technological world*
> - *build and apply a repertoire of knowledge, understanding and skills in order to design and make high-quality prototypes and products for a wide range of users*
> - *critique, evaluate and test their ideas and products and the work of others*
> - *understand and apply the principles of nutrition and learn how to cook.*
>
> *(DfE, 2013)*

It is hoped that this planning resource will provide a programme of study which is dynamic and evolving, with teachers adapting and developing the ideas in the units. This planning resource has three topics for each year, split into two, providing coverage of the National Curriculum aims and objectives. The units have been developed to provide a variety of creative, technical and practical activities to engage children in an iterative process of designing and making. Where possible extend the learning online and include visits to relevant places.

In this planning guide, the five content strands have informed the long-term planning:

Design   **Technical knowledge**
Make   **Cooking and nutrition**
Evaluate

Terminology

In this guide, the main terms used are:

- **Learning objectives**: the skills, understandings and knowledge which it is intended that children should be able to demonstrate and use at the end of the unit of work.
- **Creative, technical and practical activities**: the activities which provide the coverage of the subject content.

Assessment

Each unit gives opportunities for assessment and evaluation: opportunities to evaluate creative and practical output, mastery of techniques and increasing technical knowledge. There are also opportunities for children to evaluate each other's work and to suggest refinement and improvement. The objectives in this planning guide provide a framework of expectations. In addition it is recommended that schools create a file of children's work, providing a record of outcomes for each unit to help benchmark achievements and progress. A teacher assessment template has been included on the CD-ROM to support your on-going assessments.

Materials

Materials, equipment and tools required for the units are mentioned throughout the planning guide. However, as it is important to have all materials ready in advance of lessons, a comprehensive list for each unit is available on the CD-ROM.

Health and safety

The new Programmes of Study do not include references to safety and hygiene. Schools should continue to make sure any design and technology work is healthy, safe and hygienic, and that risk assessments are carried out prior to undertaking any projects. Teachers and support staff must be knowledgeable about all relevant aspects of health and safety and feel confident in managing a healthy and safe working environment. It is crucial that they can identify the hazards and assess the risks, and determine how to remove or control the risks within an educational environment. The Design and Technology Association (DATA) offer training and advice on this important area.

About the book

The book provides content for each year group (Years 1–6) and includes:

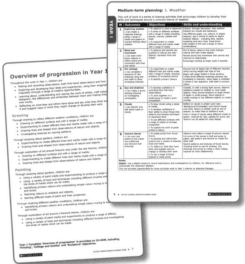

- **Long-term planning**: An overview of the National Curriculum objectives to be covered in that year (based upon the statutory guidance from the curriculum – DfE, 2013 – and supportive non-statutory guidance from DATA and other previously published guidance).
- **Overview of progression**: A year-by-year overview of how the children progress through the design and technology skills and understandings, adapted from the DATA Progression Framework (available from www.data.org.uk).
- **Medium-term planning**: Six design briefs are provided for each year group based around three topics. Each brief contains an overview of the planning in the three phases – designing, making and evaluating, including learning objectives and the creative, technical and practical activities undertaken to complete the project.
- **Background knowledge**: This explains key concepts, relevant to the projects, to help support teachers' knowledge of design and technology.

About the CD-ROM

The CD-ROM provides the long-term planning, progression, medium-term planning, background knowledge, unit materials and components lists and evaluation sheets as pdfs or editable Word files. Some design templates and supporting resources, mentioned in the planning sessions, are also provided. From the menu screen on the CD-ROM, simply navigate to the year group you require and click on the button to open the associated file. Visit **www.scholastic.co.uk/100designandtechnology** for some additional resources linked to the content of this book.

About the poster

The poster summarises the progression of key concepts and skills and techniques in the National Curriculum. Display it in a central location, such as the staffroom, to help improve understanding of the new curriculum within your school.

Year 1 Long-term planning

Design

The National Curriculum states that when designing and making, children should be taught to:
- design purposeful, functional, appealing products for themselves and other users based on design criteria
- generate, develop, model and communicate their ideas through talking, drawing, templates, mock-ups and, where appropriate, information and communication.

Design products from a range of areas, including:
- vegetable and fruit salads
- hand puppets
- paper bags
- celebration cards
- vehicles with wheels
- ice lollies
- fridge magnets.

Model and communicate their ideas through:
- discussion and surveys
- drawings, labelled diagrams and photographs
- making models
- planning and drafting
- using computers to design.

Make

The National Curriculum states that when designing and making, children should be taught to:
- select from and use a range of tools and equipment to perform practical tasks (for example, cutting, shaping, joining and finishing)
- select from and use a wide range of materials and components, including construction materials, textiles and ingredients, according to their characteristics.

Use a range of tools across each area of design technology including:
- utensils to cut and prepare food ingredients
- sewing and embroidery equipment
- scissors and glue
- hole-punch and paper drill
- printing equipment and stencils
- ICT design software
- hacksaw and jinx frames.

Use a range of materials to make their products, including:
- fruit, vegetables and fruit juices
- fabric materials and threads
- decorative materials (paint, beads, buttons, ribbons, glitter, felt pens)
- paper, card and cardboard
- wood and dowelling
- plastic wheels and cotton reels.

Evaluate

The National Curriculum states that when designing and making, children should be taught to:
- explore and evaluate a range of existing products
- evaluate their ideas and products against design criteria.

Explore and evaluate a range of products including:
- fruit, vegetables and fruit juices
- party bags and paper bags
- celebration cards
- toy vehicles with wheels
- fridge magnets.

Technical knowledge

The National Curriculum states that when designing and making, children should be taught to:
- build structures, exploring how they can be made stronger, stiffer and more stable
- explore and use mechanisms (for example, levers, sliders, wheels and axles), in their products.

Acquire technical knowledge in the following areas:
- exploring and using mechanisms including levers, slides, wheels and axles.

Cooking and nutrition

The National Curriculum states that children should be taught to:
- use the basic principles of a healthy and varied diet to prepare dishes
- understand where food comes from.

Children acquire knowledge and understanding of healthy eating by:
- designing and making salads that encourage a '5-a-day' habit
- designing and making vegetable puppets to promote a '5-a-day' habit
- designing and making ice lollies from fruit juice and real fruit pieces.
- designing and making fridge magnets to remind them to 'eat healthily'.

Overview of progression in Year 1

Designing

Throughout units of work in Year 1 children:

- use knowledge of existing products to help form ideas
- generate ideas from their own experiences
- state what products they are designing and making and what they are for
- say whether their products are for themselves or other users
- describe what their products are for and how their products will work
- say how they will make their products suitable for their intended users
- develop and communicate ideas by talking and drawing
- use simple design criteria to help develop their ideas
- model ideas by exploring materials, components and construction kits and by making templates and mock-ups
- use information and communication technology, where appropriate, to develop and communicate their ideas.

Making and technical knowledge: Cooking and nutrition

By designing and making a 5-a-day salad and fruity iced lollies, children:

- know that all food comes from plants or animals, and has to be farmed, grown elsewhere (for example, home) or caught
- know that everyone should eat at least five portions of fruit and vegetables every day
- follow procedures for safety and hygiene
- measure and weigh ingredients
- prepare and assemble a range of ingredients using techniques such as cutting, peeling and grating
- know how to prepare simple dishes safely and hygienically, without using a heat source
- use the correct technical vocabulary to describe food and ingredients, including taste, smell, texture and feel.

Making and technical knowledge: Textiles

By designing and making a hand puppet, children:

- select from a range of tools and equipment, explaining their choices
- select and use a range of textile materials according to their characteristics
- follow procedures for safety
- measure, mark out, cut, shape and join textile materials
- use finishing techniques, including those from art and design
- know that a 3D textile product can be assembled from two identical fabric shapes
- use the correct technical vocabulary to describe sewing and joining fabrics and decorations.

Year 1 Complete 'Overview of progression' is provided on the CD-ROM, including 'Making and technical knowledge: Construction', 'Making and technical knowledge: Sheet materials' and 'Evaluating' objectives.

Year 1 Medium-term planning: 1A Salads: '5-a-day' salads

Design brief: To design and make salad to encourage children to eat their '5-a-day'.

P	Learning objectives	Creative, technical and practical activities
Designing	• To know that all food comes from animals or plants. • To know that food is farmed, grown elsewhere (at home) or caught. • To understand the importance of eating five portions of fruit and vegetables every day.	**Generating, developing, modelling and communicating ideas** Know your fruit and vegetables! Provide children with a range of name and sorting activities to teach children the names of popular fruit and vegetables and to identify which are fruits and which are vegetables. Discuss and explain with children the importance of eating five portions of fruit and vegetables every day. **Evaluating existing products (EEP): Fruit and vegetables** Give the children the opportunity to develop a food vocabulary by smelling, tasting and feeling different fruits and vegetables. Create a word bank display of sensory words. Many children may not have experienced a wide range of fruit and vegetables and so setting up a daily salad/fruit bar may encourage them to eat more. Discuss with the children what their favourite fruit and vegetables are then they can carry out surveys and display results. Some suggestions would be: • favourite fruits (display as block graph or pictogram) • favourite vegetables (display as block graph or pictogram) • daily diary of fruit and vegetables eaten.
Making	• To prepare a range of dishes safely and hygienically without using a heat source. • To apply simple food preparation techniques such as cutting, grating and peeling.	**Focused practical task (FPT): Designing and making a salad** Present the children with a scenario, for example, 'The Jolly Postman only eats brightly coloured vegetable salads' or 'What salad do you think Handa would like?' As a class children decide on the fruit and vegetables they would use. Demonstrate how to make the salad, focusing on: • basic food hygiene • washing the fruit or vegetables before preparing them • preparing by grating, peeling, slicing and squeezing. **Designing** Ask children to design and make a salad for another child, to encourage them to eat five portions of fruit and vegetables every day. Discuss with children: • What would encourage children to eat more fruit and vegetables? • How can you make a salad look more interesting? Children work in pairs or small groups to decide what salad they are going to make and for whom. Is it going to be for a child in their group or a fictional character (give them a scenario)? They then decide whether to make a fruit salad, vegetable salad or mixed salad. They create a plan to make the salad: • list the fruit and vegetables they will need • list how much of each ingredient is needed • how they will prepare the ingredients • tools that they will need • jobs for each group member and order of working. They follow the plan to make the salad – encourage children to present their food attractively.
Evaluating	• To describe how a product works in simple terms.	When they have completed their product, encourage them to either draw the salad or take and print a digital photograph. As part of their evaluation, each child: • gives an exciting name for their salad (and adds this as a title to the drawing/photo) • labels the different ingredients found in the salad • writes who they designed the salad for and why it might encourage them to eat more fruit and vegetables. Introduce the children to the 'Cooking: evaluation sheet' from the CD-ROM and capture any comments from them about the tasks.

Notes:
Book references: *The Jolly Postman* by Janet and Allan Ahlberg, *Handa's Surprise* by Eileen Browne.
See background notes on teaching about a healthy diet and understanding where food comes from.

■SCHOLASTIC

Year 1 Medium-term planning: 1B Salads: Veggie puppet

Design brief: To design and make a hand puppet for a puppet show to encourage children to eat vegetables.

P	Learning objectives	Creative, technical and practical activities
Designing	• To generate ideas based on experiences of different materials, components and products. • To plan what to do based on experiences of working with different materials and components. • To use models and pictures with words to describe designs.	**Generating, developing, modelling and communicating ideas** Discuss with children which vegetables they like eating and those they do not. What is their favourite vegetable? What do they like about it? **Evaluating existing products (EEP): Puppets** Show children some hand puppets of animals. What are the similarities between the puppets? (Same basic design with head and arms.) Demonstrate where the 'puppeteer' puts their hands and fingers to control the puppet. Allow the children to experience using the puppets. Explain that the children are going to make a hand puppet of one of their favourite vegetables. Explain that each puppet will have the same basic design (show simple hand puppet template) and that children have to design their veggie puppet around that basic template shape. Lead discussion about the choices the children need to make: • Which vegetable are they going to choose? • What is the colour of the vegetable? • What is the shape of the vegetable? • How does it fit with the template? Children collect images of their vegetable. They design their puppet, firstly trying out drawn shapes, then using a sheet with basic hand puppet outline. Encourage children to make the puppet look like a vegetable and to add features such as hair and a face.
Making	• To use a range of materials and tools with help where needed. • To cut out shapes which have been created by drawing round a template onto fabric. • To join fabrics by stitching or gluing pieces together. • To use a glue gun when supervised by an adult. • To decorate fabrics with ribbons, stitches, buttons, beads and sequins.	**Focused practical tasks (FPT): Making a puppet** • Demonstrate how to draw around a card template of the hand puppet on felt to make two identical felt puppet shapes. Children select their coloured felt for the puppet and then repeat the process to create their own basic hand puppet. • Children use a range of materials to decorate each piece of the puppet – they can use stitching to secure beads, buttons and ribbons. • Demonstrate how to use a running stitch to join the two pieces of felt together to make the hand puppet. Children should practise running stitch on scrap material before joining the two pieces of their puppet. • Demonstrate how threading through and knotting lengths of wool can be used to create hair for their puppet.
Evaluating	• To recognise what has worked well during the making process. • To suggest ways of improving a product.	As part of the evaluation process, explain to the children that it is important to evaluate the puppet product by asking questions, such as: • What part did you enjoy most? • What did you find easy to do? • What did you find difficult to do? • What could have been done better? • What did you get better at? Once the class have completed their puppets, they gather in groups to write a short play about their vegetables and why it is important to eat vegetables regularly. Use the 'Product evaluation sheet' from the CD-ROM to review the project with the children.

Notes:
A puppet template can be found on the CD-ROM.
Children could use their puppet to record a short video encouraging other children to eat more fruit and vegetables.

Cross-curricular links:
PSHE: healthy eating

Year 1 Medium-term planning: 2A Celebration time: Party bags

Design brief: To design and make a goodie bag for a birthday party.

P	Learning objectives	Creative, technical and practical activities
Designing	• To generate ideas based on experiences of different materials, components and products. • To plan what to do based on experiences of working with different materials and components. • To use models and pictures with words to describe designs.	Ensure children understand what is meant by a party or goody bag. *When are they given out? What would be put in a goody bag?* Children carry out a simple survey amongst their friends to find out what they would most like to see in a party bag. Each friend chooses three items. **Investigation** Children investigate the strength of a paper bag. Give children two sheets of art paper and a stapler and challenge them to create their own paper bag with handles. Their finished product is then tested for strength and size by adding multilink cubes to see how many their bags can hold without breaking. This can be extended by asking children how they might strengthen their bag and allowing them further investigation to improve their bag. **Evaluating existing products (EEP): Gift bags** Provide a range of gift bags for children to examine. If possible allow them to attempt to disassemble them in order that they find out that they are made from one sheet of paper/card material. Children use this opportunity to look at how the handles are made and attached and how the bags are decorated (colours, images, patterns, words etc.). **Focused practical tasks (FPT)** With adult help, children make a paper bag from a single sheet of paper (see background knowledge and video link suggestion). A3 size paper should be used to create a reasonable sized bag. Use ribbon or string to create the handles, discussing the advantages of both. Additional card can be used to strengthen and secure the handles. **Designing** Children decide on a theme for their party bag and decorate it accordingly. This could be patterns, stars, flowers, pictures, animals, etc. Remind them to take care when drawing and designing and not rush.
Making	• To use a range of material and tools with help where needed. • To fold, roll, tear, curl and cut paper and card to create a range of structures. • To investigate different ways to strengthen a range of sheet materials. • To create temporary, fixed and moving joins.	Give children the opportunity to experience a variety of ways to add decoration to A3 sheets of paper, before making the bag: • potato printing • marbling • ICT paint software (A4 design will need to be enlarged to A3) • ICT combining words and clipart • stencil printing • painting or felt-tipped pens • embellishing with glitter, sequins, etc. When the A3 paper designs are completed, each child chooses which sheet to turn into a bag following the technique used in the FPT and/or background knowledge. Help children to create their bags from the sheets. Use a hole-punch to make holes for handles (and strengthen with card). Add the handles.
Evaluating	• To express a preference for a product from a range of finished items and give reasons for their choices.	Create a class display of children's party bags. If possible, include photos of children designing and making their bags. Children view the party bags and decide which ones they like best and give reasons for their choices.

Notes:
A3 sheets of printed paper, such as wrapping paper, can be used if time is limited.

Cross-curricular links:
Art and design: printing and other techniques

■ SCHOLASTIC

Year 1 Medium-term planning: 2B Celebration time: Pop-up card

Design brief: To create a range of celebration cards using simple pop-up book mechanisms.

P	Learning objectives	Creative, technical and practical activities
Designing	• To generate ideas based on experiences of different materials, components and products. • To plan what to do based on experiences of working with different materials and components. • To use models and pictures with words to describe designs.	**Evaluating existing products (EEP): Celebration cards** Collect commercially produced celebration cards and give children the opportunity in the designing phase to study them and understand what is meant by illustrations, slogans and verses. Children label the different features of celebration cards. Give children the opportunity to investigate, disassemble and discuss pop-up cards and introduce children to the correct terminology, such as fold, crease, lever and pivot. **Technical knowledge** Children use simple construction kits to explore mechanisms, such as levers and slides. **Focused practical tasks (FPT)** Teach children, through focused practical tasks, the following range of pop-up and moving mechanisms: • pop-up box (using two simple cuts across the card fold) • pop-up box with one decorative cut (pointed cut or zig-zag cut) • sliding mechanisms (appearing and disappearing) • lever mechanisms with a fixed pivot. Explain that once the mechanism has been created and tested, a picture or words are attached to the mechanism. Discuss the 'My design' sheet with the children to assist with the planning stage.
Making	• To explain what they are making and the tools they are using. • To use a range of materials and tools with help where needed. • To fold, roll, tear, curl and cut paper and card to create a range of structures. • To use simple pop-ups. • To cut a variety of lines, straight and curved. • To create temporary, fixed and moving joins.	**Planning** For each card, children: • choose a celebration as the card focus • decide on the mechanism that will be used (or give suggestion) • plan and draft the cover and inside of their card (images and words) • use ICT design software to produce images and words, if required • plan to use other finishing techniques, such as felt tipped pens, glitter, etc. Encourage children to gather together all the resources that they will need to make each card before starting. Discuss with children the order in which things need to be done. Children may need help with: • using tools and equipment safely • using a hole-punch or card drill • making a pivot using a paper fastener and ensuring that the fastener is neither too loose nor too tight.
Evaluating	• To describe how a product works in simple terms. • To recognise what has worked well during the making process. • To suggest ways of improving a product.	As children are making each card encourage them to consider what is working well and how they could improve the card. • Does the card work as they had planned? • Does the illustration move in the right direction? As the unit progresses, children will have had the opportunity to make several different cards. This gives them the chance to improve their design and their making skills. At the end of the unit allow the children to reflect on all their cards and to identify ways in which their cards have improved. Display the 'Product evaluation sheet' from the CD-ROM. Use it to review the project with the children.

Notes:
This unit of work can be delivered at any point during the year to reflect different festivals and celebrations.
Visit the Scholastic web site (www.scholastic.co.uk/100designandtechnology) for a 'pop-up card' activity on the theme of fireworks.

Cross-curricular links:
English: text for celebration cards

Year 1 Medium-term planning: 3A Summer time: Summer buggies

Design brief: To design and make a model of a vehicle to transport you and three other people to the seaside.

P	Learning objectives	Creative, technical and practical activities
Designing	• To generate ideas based on experiences of different materials, components and products. • To use models and pictures with words to describe designs. • To make vehicles with construction kits which contain free running wheels. • To attach wheels to a chassis using an axle. • To cut strip wood/dowel using hacksaw and bench hook.	Children learn how wheels and axles work by making their own vehicle. **Generating, developing, modelling and communicating ideas** Discuss the different types of transport children know. *How do you get to school? How do people get to the seaside?* (Car, bus, coach, train, bike.) Show images of a range of vehicles. Can children name the vehicles? *How many have wheels? How many wheels does each vehicle have? Are these wheels all the same size?* Extend discussion to look at how transport has changed over time. Provide a collection of toy vehicles, give children time to investigate: focus their attention on the wheels and axles. Ask them to draw vehicles, labelling the wheels and axles. **Technical knowledge** Children use simple construction kits to explore how wheels and axles are put together to make moving vehicles before beginning their own design and make task. **Focused practical task (FPT)** Demonstrate how to make a vehicle chassis using 10mm square lengths of wood, jinx blocks and card triangles to strengthen the chassis. Use card triangles to attach axles to the chassis. Each child makes a chassis (to the size of a cereal box). **Designing** Explain the brief, to design and make a model of a vehicle to take four people to the seaside. Models will be made from a cereal box attached to the chassis. Show children the range of materials that they will be working with. Children to consider the following and include on their design sheet: • What kind of vehicle will you make? What will it look like? • How many wheels will it have? • Where will you and your passengers sit? • What materials will you need to make it? • In what order will you make the parts of the vehicle? Ask children to draw their design and label the main parts using the correct vocabulary.
Making	• To use a range of materials to create models with wheels and axles, for example, tubes, dowel, cotton reels. • To join appropriately for different materials and situations, for example, glue and tape.	Encourage children to follow their design sheet and use just the materials provided for the task. When the chassis and main body are completed, provide children with images and examples of vehicles and ask them to focus on and discuss additional features such as: steering wheels, door handles, exhaust pipes, windows, etc. Task children with adding some additional features to add realism to their model and provide a better quality finish. Explain that in the real world designers review their designs whilst they work to improve the product.
Evaluating	• To describe how a product works in simple terms. • To recognise what has worked well during the making process. • To suggest ways of improving a product.	**Discussion: What makes a good vehicle?** Take suggestions and list them – explain that these can be used to measure the success of their model. Children assess their model against these criteria, in discussion with a friend. Further discuss how using and agreeing these criteria would have helped during the design phase. Children return to their original design drawing and suggest improvements that they would now make (using the design criteria) and add any additional features.

Notes:

Prior to undertaking the unit, ask children to safely photograph or find images of as many forms of transport as possible, to use in the discussion.

Cross-curricular links:

Humanities: history of transport and/or seaside holidays

Year 1 Medium-term planning: 3B Summer time:
Something for the fridge

Design brief: To design and make fruity ice lollies and 'eatwell' fridge magnets.

P	Learning objectives	Creative, technical and practical activities
Designing	• To generate ideas based on experiences of different materials, components and products. • To sort groups into five groups according to 'The eatwell plate'. • To understand the importance of eating five portions of fruit and vegetables every day.	**Fridge magnets** **Generating, developing, modelling and communicating ideas** Children discuss their favourite foods and draw pictures of them. They are introduced to 'The eatwell plate'. *What are good foods to eat?* Children match pictures of their favourite foods to 'The eatwell plate'. **Discussion: How could you be reminded each day to eat healthy foods?** Take suggestions and then introduce the idea of fridge magnets. **Evaluating existing products (EEP): Fridge magnets** Show some fridge magnets in case children are unfamiliar with them. *What is a fridge magnet?* (A picture and/or a message with a magnet on the back.) ***Fruity ice lollies*** Remind children of the importance of eating five portions of fruit and/or vegetables a day. **Evaluating existing products (EEP): Squashes** Taste test different orange juices and orange squash. Which do they prefer? Taste test different flavours of fruit juices. Which do they prefer? *Which flavours work well together?* Test other juices, e.g. tomato or carrot. *Which would make a good iced lolly?* **Designing** Which juice would they choose to use for their lolly, and why? How can the lolly be more attractive? (layers of flavours, actual pieces of real fruit.) Show children a lolly mould and ask them to draw what their ice lolly will look like when frozen. Children label the flavours and/or cut pieces. Introduce the 'Cooking: designing and making' sheet from the CD-ROM to the children. Discuss with the children and use it to plan the projects.
Making	• To explain what they are making and the tools they are using. • To prepare a range of dishes safely and hygienically without using a heat source. • To apply simple food preparation techniques such as cutting, grating and peeling. • To use a range of materials and tools with help where needed. • To cut a variety of lines, straight and curved.	**Making the fridge magnets** • Using ICT paint software children create pictures of healthy food for their fridge magnets. • Then using a word processor type the names of chosen food in a range of fonts. (Using ICT allows editing of pictures and words.) • Print out preferred designs and then cut them out. Suggest children layer names and words on top of the images. • Laminate and cut out designs, with adult help. • Add small magnets or a piece of magnetic strip to the back of the designs to complete the magnet. **Making the fruity ice lollies** • If children are adding pieces of fruit to their lolly, demonstrate how to cut and chop the fruit into small pieces first children do so. • If children are producing a layered effect they will need to leave time to let each layer freeze. (Lolly moulds should be labelled with each child's name.).
Evaluating	• To describe how a product works in simple terms. • To recognise what has worked well during the making process.	**Evaluating their own ideas and products** Children evaluate their fridge magnet by answering questions, such as: • Does the fridge magnet stick to the fridge? • Is the picture clear and can you tell what type of food it is? • Are the words clear and spelled correctly? • Is the fridge magnet a healthy food? How do you know? Children taste and evaluate their own ice lolly by answering questions, such as: • Does your ice lolly taste/look nice? What is the best part of it? • Would you buy one of your ice lollies from a shop?

Notes:
The 'fruit and veg plate' (or the 'eatwell plate' referenced above) can be found on the CD-ROM.
Children could be asked to bring in examples of fridge magnets from home. (Check before displaying!)

Cross-curricular links:
PSHE: healthy eating; Science: magnets

Year 1 Background knowledge

Salads: '5-a-day' salads

Children in Years 1 and 2 should name and sort foods into the five groups from 'The eatwell plate':

- fruit and vegetables
- meat, fish, eggs, beans
- bread, rice potatoes and pasta
- milk and dairy foods
- food and drink high in fats and/or sugar.

They should be taught that a healthy diet comprises food and drink from the food groups and that everyone should eat at least five portions of fruit and vegetables every day.

Children should be taught that all food comes from plants and animals and that food has to be farmed, caught or grown elsewhere (at home, school, allotment).

Internet search www.gov.uk 'The eatwell plate' for further information and resources.

Video resource:

BBC Learning Website – Design Technology Video: *The importance of food presentation* and *Why do we need to eat fruit and vegetables?*

Website recommendation: www.freshforkids.com.au

Salads: Veggie puppet

Video resource: BBC Learning Website – Design Technology Video:
Putting on a puppet show (parts 1 & 2)

Basic template design for a hand puppet

Celebration time: Party bags

Paper carrier bag (video available on Youtube 'How to make a paper bag' by 123peppy.com)

1. Fold the paper in half and score to make a proper crease.

2. On the opposite open side, fold over approximately 1cm and score the fold.

3. Use glue to secure the out and middle part of the fold to the paper and trim this down.

4. Measure approximately 3cm in on each side of the paper.

5. Use a ruler to help fold these sides over and firm the crease.

6. Open up the folds and reverse them on each side to create an open cuboid.

Base of the bag:

1. Select one end as the base, fold over approximately 1cm and score the fold.

2. Secure with glue and firm down.

3. Fold this over again, approximately 4cm and score with a ruler.

4. Open up this fold and reverse to create the base of the bag.

Use a hole-punch to make holes at the top and use string or ribbon to for the handles.

Weblink: http://www.paperworks.ebcnet.co.uk for information on paper and curriculum linked learning resources.

■SCHOLASTIC

Year 2 Long-term planning

Design

The National Curriculum states that when designing and making, children should be taught to:
- design purposeful, functional, appealing products for themselves and other users based on design criteria
- generate, develop, model and communicate their ideas through talking, drawing, templates, mock-ups and, where appropriate, information and communication.

Design products from a range of areas, including:
- sandwiches
- pulley systems and winding mechanisms
- wall hangings and embroidery
- breakfast cereals
- toy clothes.

Model and communicate their ideas through:
- discussion and taste testing surveys
- drawings and labelled diagrams
- instructions and recipes
- lists
- letter writing
- action plans.

Make

The National Curriculum states that when designing and making, children should be taught to:
- select from and use a range of tools and equipment to perform practical tasks (for example, cutting, shaping, joining and finishing)
- select from and use a wide range of materials and components, including construction materials, textiles and ingredients, according to their characteristics.

Use a range of tools across each area of design technology including:
- utensils to cut and prepare food ingredients
- sewing and embroidery equipment
- scissors and card snips
- PVA glue and glue gun
- hacksaw and bench hook.

Use a range of materials to make their products, including:
- range of breads, spreads and sandwich fillings
- sheet materials, paper, cards and cardboard
- recycled boxes, cylinders and other junk materials
- construction kits with wheels and pulleys
- wooden strips and 10mm lengths
- decorative materials (paint, beads, buttons, ribbons, glitter, felt pens)
- fabrics, calico and felt
- embroidery threads
- fabric paints and pens.

Evaluate

The National Curriculum states that when designing and making, children should be taught to:
- explore and evaluate a range of existing products
- evaluate their ideas and products against design criteria.

Explore and evaluate a range of products including:
- sandwiches
- breads and spreads
- porridge products
- waistcoats.

Technical knowledge

The National Curriculum states that when designing and making, children should be taught to:
- build structures, exploring how they can be made stronger, stiffer and more stable
- explore and use mechanisms (for example, levers, sliders, wheels and axles), in their products.

Acquire technical knowledge in the following areas:
- explore and use mechanisms including wheels and axles
- build structures and make them stronger, stiffer and more stable.

Cooking and nutrition

The National Curriculum states that children should be taught to:
- use the basic principles of a healthy and varied diet to prepare dishes
- understand where food comes from.

Children acquire knowledge and understanding of healthy eating by:
- designing different sandwich fillings and choosing the types of bread and spread to use
- designing a new topping for the three bears' porridge using fruit, nuts or honey.

Overview of progression in Year 2

Designing

Throughout units of work in Year 2 children:

- use knowledge of existing products to help form ideas
- generate ideas from their own experiences
- state what products they are designing and making and what they are for
- say whether their products are for themselves or other users
- describe what their products are for and how their products will work
- say how they will make their products suitable for their intended users
- develop and communicate ideas by talking and drawing
- use simple design criteria to help develop their ideas
- model ideas by exploring materials, components and construction kits and by making templates and mock-ups
- use information and communication technology, where appropriate, to develop and communicate their ideas.

Making and technical knowledge: Cooking and nutrition

By designing and making picnic sandwiches and porridge, children:

- know that all food comes from plants or animals, and has to be farmed, grown elsewhere (for example, at home) or caught
- know how to name and sort foods into the five groups
- know that everyone should eat at least five portions of fruit and vegetables every day
- follow procedures for safety and hygiene
- measure and weigh ingredients
- prepare and assemble a range of ingredients using techniques such as cutting, peeling and grating
- know how to prepare simple dishes safely and hygienically, without using a heat source
- use the correct technical vocabulary to describe food and ingredients, including taste, smell, texture and feel.

Making and technical knowledge: Textiles

By designing and making wall hangings for a great hall, children:

- select from a range of tools and equipment, explaining their choices
- select and use a range of textile materials according to their characteristics
- follow procedures for safety
- measure, mark out, cut, shape and join textile materials
- use finishing techniques, including those from art and design
- know that a 3D textile product can be assembled from two identical fabric shapes
- use the correct technical vocabulary to describe sewing and joining fabrics and decorations.

Year 2 Complete 'Overview of progression' is provided on the CD-ROM, including 'Making and technical knowledge: Construction', 'Making and technical knowledge: Sheet materials' and 'Evaluating' objectives.

Year 2 Medium-term planning: 1A *The Lighthouse Keeper's Lunch*: Picnic sandwiches

Design brief: To design and make some picnic sandwiches for the lighthouse keeper's lunch.

P	Learning objectives	Creative, technical and practical activities
Designing	• To plan what to do based on experiences of working with different materials and components. • To use models and pictures with words to describe designs. • To know that all food comes from animals or plants. • To know that food is either farmed, grown elsewhere (at home) or caught.	**Discussion: What is your favourite sandwich?** Discuss various sandwiches with children then ask them to decide on their favourite sandwich to eat. Ask them to draw their sandwich, considering the three parts (bread, spread and filling): • What type of bread do you prefer? • What type of spread do you prefer? • What type of filling are you going to use? **Evaluating existing products (EEP): Breads and spreads** Children make a list of the different types of spreads that can be used in sandwiches (butter, margarine, dairy spread and mayonnaise, etc.). They then list as many different types of breads that they know of that are used for sandwiches. Conduct a class 'taste test', test a range of breads combined with different spreads and decide which they like the best and the least. Introduce and discuss the design brief. *Which type of sandwich would the lighthouse keeper prefer?* Make a list of as many different sandwich fillings as they can and collate as a class. Discuss the types of fillings and where they come from. For example: • strawberry jam: from strawberries that are the fruit of a plant • fish paste: from fish which are caught in the sea • cheese: made from milk which comes from cows which are reared on a farm. Extend the discussion to discuss combinations of fillings that work well. What are the traditional combinations? (tuna and cucumber, cheese and onion, etc.) If time permits, a further evaluation can be carried out in which different fillings are taste tested (useful if some children are not sandwich eaters). **Designing** Children design a sandwich that the lighthouse keeper would like. They draw the sandwich and label the type of: • bread to be used • spread to be used • filling to be used. They list the equipment that they will need to make the sandwich and write a set of instructions to make the sandwich using the 'Cooking: designing and making sheet' from the CD-ROM.
Making	• To explain what they are making and the tools they are using. • To prepare a range of dishes safely and hygienically without using a heat source. • To apply simple food preparation techniques such as cutting, grating and peeling.	Before beginning, children discuss how they are going to work safely and hygienically. In pairs, children prepare the ingredients and tools and equipment they will need to make their sandwiches, checking each other's instructions. They make their sandwiches following their set of instructions.
Evaluating	• To describe how a product works in simple terms. • To recognise what has worked well during the making process. • To suggest ways of improving their product.	**Evaluating their own ideas and products** Children take a photograph of their finished product and compare it to their design drawing. In small groups, children should have the opportunity to taste small samples of each other's finished sandwich product. They evaluate the sandwich either through: • happy/sad face • by choosing the best sandwich • by giving marks out of ten • sorting into like and dislike. Children should also have the opportunity to evaluate their own sandwich in more detail commenting upon whether they liked it or not (and giving reasons) and how they might improve their sandwich design next time.

Notes:
This unit of work is based on the children's book *The Lighthouse Keeper's Lunch* by Ronda and David Armitage. Care should be taken with the 'taste test' particularly with regard to vegetarians and religious observance.

Year 2 Medium-term planning: 1B *The Lighthouse Keeper's Lunch*: Pulleys

Design brief: To design a simple mechanism to deliver the lighthouse keeper's lunch.

P	Learning objectives	Creative, technical and practical activities
Designing	• To generate ideas based on experiences of different materials, components and products. • To plan what to do based on experiences of working with different materials and components according to their characteristics. • To use models and pictures with words to describe designs.	This unit of work builds upon children's previous work with wheels and axles. It allows the children to explore a simple pulley mechanism and then use this knowledge when applying it to their own design and making project. Working in groups and using a range of sheet materials and recycled material, children create a large model of the lighthouse using images from the story *The Lighthouse Keeper's Lunch* for ideas. The model should be securely fastened to a large base. **Technical knowledge** Children use simple construction kits to explore simple pulley mechanisms before beginning their own design and make task. **Focused practical task (FPT)** Children experiment with pulley systems and investigate the effects of having different-sized wheels and the speed of these wheels. They learn that fixing an object to a point on the pulley belt allows the object to be moved when the pulleys are rotated. **Designing** Provide children with an outline image of a lighthouse. Ask them to design a pulley system to transport a basket of sandwiches from the base to the top of the lighthouse. Suggest they label the pulleys, pulley belt, basket, supports, axle and handle. They should also indicate the direction of turn of the pulleys and the direction in which the basket will travel. This design sheet will form the basis of their group's work. Give each group a copy of the 'My design sheet' from the CD-ROM to help plan their work.
Making	• To explain what they are making and the tools they are using. • To use a range of materials and tools with help where needed. • To use a range of materials to create models with wheels and axles, e.g. tubes, dowel, cotton reels. • To join appropriately for different materials and situations e.g. glue and tape. • To mark out materials to be cut using a template. • To cut strip wood/dowel using a hacksaw and bench hook. • To use a glue gun when supervised by an adult.	In groups, children choose which of the individual designs they will use. Or they may decide to incorporate the best elements of several designs. **Creating the pulley mechanism** The support structure should be made from wooden strips with dowelling and ready-made pulley wheels. The pulley belt can be made from an elastic band or tight string/cotton thread. **Making the basket** Children design and make the basket to keep the sandwiches safe.
Evaluating	• To describe how a product works in simple terms. • To recognise what has worked well during the making process. • To suggest ways of improving a model or product.	**Evaluating their own ideas and products** Children take a digital photograph of the finished model. They label all the parts of the pulley mechanism, including arrows to show the direction of movement. They write sentences to describe: • how the model work (does it safely transport the sandwiches to the top of the lighthouse?) • which parts of the project they most enjoyed doing • how they could improve their own design based on their experience of working in a group to make the model.

Notes:

This unit of work is based on the children's book *The Lighthouse Keeper's Lunch* by Ronda and David Armitage. This work can be extended by creating a simple circuit with a flashing bulb and switch that can be added to the lighthouse model to add further realism.

Year 2 Medium-term planning: 2A Castles:
Drawbridge and castle toy

Design brief: To design and make a drawbridge for a toy castle.

P	Learning objectives	Creative, technical and practical activities
Designing	• To generate ideas based on experiences of different materials, components and products. • To plan what to do based on experiences of working with different materials and components according to their characteristics. • To use models and pictures with words to describe designs.	This unit of work builds upon children's previous work with wheels and axles. It allows the children to explore a simple winding mechanism and then use this knowledge when applying it to their own design and making project. **Technical knowledge** Children use simple construction kits to explore simple winding mechanisms before beginning their own design and make task. They explore how to strengthen and stiffen card using diagonal struts and/or by folding and layering card. **Focused practical task (FPT)** Demonstrate to children how to make a simple winding mechanism by: • fixing two cotton reels to a length of dowel so that they do not move • attaching thread to the cotton reels and then attaching an object to the end of the thread • turning the axle so that the thread is wound around the cotton reels and the object is lifted. Children create their winding mechanism, then: • show how clothes pegs hold the axle but also allow them to rotate • develop this idea to demonstrate how a drawbridge works. Show children a simple drawbridge mechanism to help them with this. **Designing** Children draw their design for a drawbridge using a cereal box for a frame and materials as above. Ask them to label the: axle, pulley, drawbridge, support, handle and pivot. They then make a list of the materials that they will need using the 'My design sheet' from the CD-ROM.
Making	• To explain what they are making and the tools they are using. • To use a range of materials to create models with wheels and axles, e.g. tubes, dowel, cotton reels. • To join appropriately for different materials and situations, e.g. glue/tape. • To cut strip wood/dowel using hacksaw and bench hook. • To know how freestanding structures can be made stronger, stiffer and more stable.	Children use their design sheet as a guide to make their drawbridge mechanism. Points to note when making the drawbridge: • the archway should be cut out of the cereal box first • clothes pegs are used to support both the axle of the pulley system and also the pivot of the drawbridge; they can be fixed to the cereal packet using a glue gun • the actual drawbridge should be made out of thin card that has been stiffened and strengthened through additional struts and a layer of folded card. Once the drawbridge mechanism has been created, test it to ensure that it works. The next stage is to decorate the drawbridge to create a castle effect: • add battlements by drawing and then cutting out shapes from sheet card • add towers from cardboard cylinders or cuboids (and add battlements) • paint with thick grey paint and allow to dry • when dry, add 'brick effect' by using thick black marker pens. This can be further developed into a complete toy castle by using a large cardboard box.
Evaluating	• To describe how a product works in simple terms. • To recognise what has worked well during the making process. • To suggest ways of improving the product.	As part of the evaluation process children assess: • How well the drawbridge works – is it easy to raise and lower? • What materials were easy to work with? • Which techniques were effective and which do they need to develop and practise more? Using their experiences of making the drawbridge, the children are now challenged to design a working portcullis for their castle.

Notes:
The additional portcullis activity is a design activity in which children build upon previous learning and are not required to make. Further details of this activity can be found in *Hot Topics: Castles* (Scholastic)
Visit the Scholastic web site (www.scholastic.co.uk/100designandtechnology) to visit an interactive medieval castle.

Cross-curricular links:
History: castles, the Norman invasion, the Battle of Hastings

Year 2 Medium-term planning: 2B Castles: In the great hall

YEAR 2

Design brief: To design and make a wall hanging to decorate the great hall of a Norman castle.

P	Learning objectives	Creative, technical and practical activities
Designing	• To generate ideas based on experiences of different materials, components and products. • To plan what to do based on experiences of working with different materials and components. • To use models and pictures with words to describe designs.	**Generating, developing, modelling and communicating ideas** If children are already learning about the Normans and castles they may well have enough ideas to create their wall hanging (tapestry); if not collect images, books and artefacts for them to study. They can be shown examples of tapestries typical of the period, such as the Bayeux Tapestry. **Focused practical task (FPT): Decorative stitching** Explain to the children that the border of their wall hanging is to be decorated with embroidery stitching. Using a sheet of Binca, show children a range of cross-stitch border designs that can be made by changing the type of stitch and the colour of threads. Give them time to practise these designs and to experiment in creating some border designs of their own. When completed, suggest they evaluate their border designs and choose which designs they will use. **Designing** Using images or drawings, children create a picture that depicts a castle scene from Norman England. Suggest that the picture has a background, with trees and clouds, and contains historical elements such as a castle, knights, horses, etc. (Children can use ready-made templates of horses, knights, castles, towers etc. cut out from card or printed from free images available online to draw around.)
Making	• To explain what they are making and the tools they are using. • To colour fabrics using fabric paints. • To use a range of material and tools with help where needed. • To cut out shapes which have been created by drawing round a template onto the fabric. • To join fabrics by stitching or gluing pieces together. • To decorate fabrics with ribbons, stitches, buttons, beads and sequins.	Using their design as a guide, children assemble their images and tools, then plan their wall hanging image on the white calico hanging (each child has an A3 sheet of white calico). The stages in making the wall hanging are: 1. The background is created using fabric paints and pens. 2. A background of embroidered cross-stitch is added to the edge of the calico. 3. The main features of the wall hanging are created out of coloured felt which are either drawn by the children or they use pre-prepared templates to draw around. 4. Elements such as the castle (with windows, doors and coloured spires) are prepared and assembled away from the wall hanging and stuck together using PVA glue. Additional embroidery decorations can be added to these features. 5. All elements are joined to the calico background using PVA glue. 6. Additional decorations (beads, ribbons, braids, etc.) are glued on to complete it. 7. Finally, additional small squares of calico are sewn to the top edge of the wall hanging and looped over a suitable sized piece of dowelling and then secured through more sewing to allow the cloth to hang. The same can be repeated at the bottom of the wall hanging.
Evaluating	• To recognise what has worked well during the making process. • To suggest ways of improving their product.	**Evaluating their own ideas and products** Compares the final product with the original design and lists ways in which it is similar and note changes that were made during the making process. Children explain why they made those changes and whether they improved the final product using the 'Product evaluation sheet' from the CD-ROM.

Notes:
See background knowledge to find out more about wall hangings and tapestries. *Hot Topics: Castles* (Scholastic) is a good source of information for these activities.

Cross-curricular links:
History: castles, the Norman invasion, the Battle of Hastings

20 ■ 100 DESIGN & TECHNOLOGY LESSONS PLANNING GUIDE ■SCHOLASTIC

Year 2 Medium-term planning: 3A *Goldilocks and the Three Bears*: Porridge

Design brief: To create a new porridge breakfast for one of the three bears.

P	Learning objectives	Creative, technical and practical activities
Designing	• To know that all food comes from animals or plants. • To know that food is either farmed, grown elsewhere (at home) or caught. • To understand the importance of eating five portions of fruit and vegetables every day.	**Discussion: Who had breakfast this morning?** Discuss the importance of having breakfast with the class. What types of food do the children have for breakfast (link to 'The eatwell plate'). Conduct a class or school breakfast survey: • What types of cereals do you eat? • What do you spread on your toast? • What fruit juices do you prefer? Provide opportunities for taste tests on cereals, fruit juices and different spreads. Draw graphs of the results of each survey. Use the 'Cooking: evaluation sheet' to record their findings. **Porridge for breakfast?** Explain to children how porridge can be made from oats and milk. They should understand that milk and oats are produced on a farm. *Who likes porridge? Who has ever eaten porridge?* Make porridge in a range of ways and ask the children to rank them in order: • made with milk • made with water • made with half milk and half water • with sugar added • with salt added. Ask children to sequence a set of instructions to make a recipe for porridge. **Evaluating existing products (EEP): Porridge** Investigate a range of products (or visiting a local supermarket) so that children understand that there are a range of porridge products that have added ingredients to enhance the flavour. Taste test or sample a range of porridges with added ingredients and choose which one they liked best. This can be linked to simple data handling activities. **Designing** *What do bears eat?* Make a list of possible foods: fruit, nuts and honey. Consider how to prepare the added ingredients by cutting, chopping, grating and mixing.
Making	• To explain what they are making and the tools they are using. • To prepare a range of dishes safely and hygienically without using a heat source. • To apply simple food preparation techniques such as cutting, grating and peeling.	Ask children to explain why it is important to wash their hands before preparing the food. Children prepare their added ingredients. Ask them to explain how they are preparing their ingredients using vocabulary such as: cutting, chopping, grating and mixing. Make a batch of porridge that is shared amongst the class so that children can add their own pre-prepared ingredients. Suggest children explain how the porridge has been made and what their added ingredients were to a partner.
Evaluating	• To say which product they preferred from a range of products and use simple explanations to explain their choice.	**Evaluating their own ideas and products** In small groups, children taste each other's porridge recipe and choose which one they liked best and they explain why. Their reasons are recorded by an adult and added to a whole class display about the project. Children write, or draw, their own recipe based on their sequenced instructions and add their own ingredients, including how to prepare them. Children write a letter to Goldilocks explaining about the new porridge for the three bears and enclosing a copy of the recipe for her to use.

Notes:
See background notes for Year 1, giving information about a healthy diet and understanding where food comes from.

Cross-curricular links:
PSHE: healthy living and the importance of breakfast
English: to enhance this unit, through shared writing, children write a sequel to the story of 'Goldilocks and the Three Bears' in which Goldilocks stays with the bears and prepares them some different porridge recipes.

Year 2 Medium-term planning: 3B *Goldilocks and the Three Bears*: Waistcoat

Design brief: To design and make a waistcoat for one of the three bears.

P	Learning objectives	Creative, technical and practical activities
Designing	• To generate ideas based on experiences of different materials, components and products. • To plan what to do based on experiences of working with different materials and components. • To use models and pictures with words to describe designs.	The design brief is to make a waistcoat for one of the three bears. If possible, provide three teddy bears as 'models' for the children (large, medium and small). **Evaluating existing products (EEP): Waistcoats** • Show the examples of waistcoats or images to the children in order that they understand what a waistcoat is. • If possible, dissemble a waistcoat to show that it is created from three separate pieces. Lay them out flat. **Investigation** Give each small group of children a teddy bear and ask them to make a paper waistcoat for the teddy using art paper and sticky tape/staples. They can make several versions but should be encouraged to use only three pieces of paper and to make sure that the waistcoat is a good fit. **Focused practical tasks (FPT)** • Children practise running stitch on a small sample of material. • Children practise backstitch on a small sample of material (optional). • Show children how to make a button hole (a slit in the material which isn't sewn) and attach a button to the sample of material. **Designing** Provide children with an outline of a teddy bear (front and back). Children use this to draw a waistcoat on to the teddy bear and to think about how they will decorate it. Children should include buttons as a form of fastening on their waistcoat design.
Making	• To explain what they are making and the tools they are using. • To use a range of materials and tools with help where needed. • To cut out shapes which have been created by drawing round a template onto the fabric. • To join fabrics by stitching or gluing pieces together. • To decorate fabrics with ribbons, stitches, buttons, beads and sequins.	Before beginning the making process, children should make a list to show the order in which they are going to create their waistcoat. Children cut out the felt using a waistcoat template. They can use a ready-made template or they can disassemble their paper waistcoat from the investigation and use this as a guide to creating their own template for their teddy. They sew the pieces together using running stitch and or backstitch. They sew a button on and make the button hole. They decorate the waistcoat using 3D fabric pens or paints following the design sheet.
Evaluating	• To describe how a product works in simple terms. • To recognise what has worked well during the making process.	Children write a letter to Goldilocks. In the letter they write a short set of instructions, with pictures, to tell Goldilocks how to make the waistcoat for one of the three bears. They tell Goldilocks what they enjoyed about the project and which parts were the most difficult. They include a photograph of the finished product, modelled by their teddy bear.

Notes:
Provide a collection of waistcoats in different styles, colours and sizes for the children to investigate, or images of waistcoats.

Cross-curricular links:
English: Children add to their 'Goldilocks and the Three Bears' sequel by describing the bears new waistcoats.

Year 2 Background knowledge

The lighthouse keeper's lunch: Picnic sandwiches

The Lighthouse Keeper's Lunch by Ronda and David Armitage (Scholastic)

There are a number of sequels to this story that feature other adventures for the lighthouse keeper.

As additional activities, children could write recipes for some of the other food that Mrs Grinling made for her husband.

Video resource: BBC Learning Website – Design Technology Video: Designing a sandwich.

The lighthouse keeper's lunch: Pulleys

Construction kits to explore winding up and pulley mechanisms are available from many educational suppliers as class sets. They consist of dowelling lengths, pulleys, strings and clothes pegs (to hold the dowelling securely in place).

For further information about pulleys and levers at Key Stage 1: http://www.freebookez.net/ks1-levers-and-pulleys-resources/

For further information about mechanisms and how they work: www.robives.com

Castles: Drawbridge and toy castle

Construction kits to explore winding up and pulley mechanisms are available from many educational suppliers as class sets. They consist of dowelling lengths, pulleys, strings and clothes pegs (to hold the dowelling securely in place).

Although this unit of work is based upon castle drawbridges, it can easily be adapted to suit other topics such as a wishing well or ships anchor.

Castles: In the great hall

The Bayeux Tapestry is not actually a tapestry it is an embroidery.

www.bayeuxtapestry.org.uk

There are only a few examples of Norman wall hangings available, but there are many from the medieval period in Europe. There are a famous set of tapestries on display at Hampton Court which have recently been conserved, a film about them is available at: http://www.hrp.org.uk/aboutus/whatwedo/collectionscare/vrtapestrieshamptoncourt.

To find examples of tapestries and wall hangings to display for children, search online for 'images of medieval tapestries' or 'images of castle wall hangings'.

Year 3 Long-term planning

Design

The National Curriculum states that when designing and making, children should be taught to:
- use research and develop design criteria to inform the design of innovative, functional, appealing products that are fit for purpose, aimed at particular individuals or groups
- generate, develop, model and communicate their ideas through discussion, annotated sketches, cross-sectional and exploded diagrams, prototypes, pattern pieces and computer-aided design.

Research a range of areas to inform their designing and making process, including:
- characters from children's books by Roald Dahl
- different types of bread
- photo frames
- pop-up books and other paper mechanisms
- Ancient Egyptian jewellery and Cleopatra.

Model and communicate their ideas through:
- drawings, illustrations and photographs
- using a standardised design sheet to convey ideas
- labelled diagrams
- action plans
- role play
- presenting their finished product to a group of friends.

Make

The National Curriculum states that when designing and making, children should be taught to:
- select from and use a wider range of tools and equipment to perform practical tasks (for example, cutting, shaping, joining and finishing) accurately
- select from and use a wider range of materials and components, including construction materials, textiles and ingredients, according to their functional properties and aesthetic qualities.

Use a range of tools across design and technology areas including:
- utensils to cut and prepare food ingredients
- food processing equipment
- scissors, card snips, sticky tape and a stapler
- craft knife and glue gun
- hole punch and paper drill
- sewing equipment.

Use a range of materials to make their products, including
- paper, card and cardboard
- decorative materials (paint, feathers, glitter, sequins, acrylic jewels, etc.)
- sheet materials, including clear acetate
- fabric materials.

Evaluate

The National Curriculum states that when designing and making, children should be taught to:
- investigate and analyse a range of existing products
- evaluate their ideas and products against their own design criteria and consider the views of others to improve their work
- understand how key events and individuals in design and technology have helped shape the world.

Investigate and evaluate a range of products including:
- soups and smoothies
- photo frames
- types of bread and rolls
- pop-up and mechanical books.

Gain a better understanding of how design and technology have shaped the world in which we live through:
- learning about designers and design companies and how household furnishings changed in the late 20th century.

Technical knowledge

The National Curriculum states that when designing and making, children should be taught to:
- apply their understanding of how to strengthen, stiffen and reinforce more complex structures
- understand and use mechanical systems in their products (for example, gears, pulleys, cams, levers and linkages)
- apply their understanding of computing to program, monitor and control their products.

Develop and consolidate technical knowledge in the following areas:
- joining sheet materials together using a range of different methods
- cutting sheet materials accurately using a craft knife.

Cooking and nutrition

The National Curriculum states that children should be taught to:
- understand and apply the principles of a healthy and varied diet
- prepare and cook a variety of predominantly savoury dishes using a range of cooking techniques
- understand seasonality, and know where and how a variety of ingredients are grown, reared, caught and processed.

Develop and consolidate their knowledge and understanding of healthy eating and nutrition by:
- designing and making soups and smoothies that use plenty of fruit and vegetables
- developing good practice in preparing food safely and hygienically
- understanding how to make bread and the role of yeast in bread-making.

Overview of progression in Year 3

Designing

Throughout units of work in Year 3 children:

- investigate similar products to get ideas, list key features and understand how they work
- describe the purpose of their products
- list design features that will appeal to intended users
- explain how parts and whole of products work and how it will be made
- research information about the needs and wants of users
- develop design criteria to inform ideas
- use prototypes and pattern pieces.

Making and technical knowledge: Cooking and nutrition

By designing and making a soup or smoothie based on a Roald Dahl character plus making bread rolls for a royal breakfast, children:

- select suitable tools and equipment
- list the order of the main stages of making
- know how to prepare and cook a variety of predominantly savoury dishes safely and hygienically including, the use of a heat source
- know how to use a range of techniques such as mixing, spreading, kneading and baking
- measure food ingredients with increasing accuracy
- apply a range of finishing techniques, with increasing accuracy.

Making and technical knowledge: Textiles

By designing and making Cleopatra's cushion, children:

- select suitable tools and equipment, materials and components
- explain choice of tools and equipment depending on skills and techniques to be used
- list the order of the main stages of making
- follow procedures for safety
- measure, mark out, cut and shape textile materials and components with increasing accuracy
- assemble, join and combine materials and components with increasing accuracy
- apply a range of finishing techniques, with increasing accuracy
- use technical vocabulary correctly and with increasing regularity to describe sewing techniques and fabrics
- know that a single fabric shape can be used to make 3D textiles products; that 3D textiles product can be made from a combination of fabric shapes.

Year 3 Complete 'Overview of progression' is provided on the CD-ROM, including 'Making and technical knowledge: Construction', 'Making and technical knowledge: Sheet materials' and 'Evaluating' objectives.

Year 3 Medium-term planning: 1A Roald Dahl: Swampy, soupy, smoothies

Design brief: To design and make a soup and a smoothie based on a Roald Dahl character.

P	Learning objectives	Creative, technical and practical activities
Designing	• To follow a recipe. • To know the types of food that are grown (fruit, vegetables and cereals). • To know that food is processed into ingredients for cooking. • To write a recipe. • To know that a recipe can be adapted to change the taste, appearance and smell.	Give the children the opportunity to follow recipes and associate them with the characters or a story written by Roald Dahl. If possible, write up ideas on the whiteboard so that they can be referred to later. • Fizzy Lifting Drinks (*Charlie and the Chocolate Factory*) • Peach Juice (*James and the Giant Peach*) • Green Pea Soup (*The Witches*) **Generating, developing, modelling and communicating ideas** Discuss where fruit and vegetables come from. *Of the fruit and vegetables available to use how many come from the UK? Which countries do other fruit and vegetables come from?* As a whole class, discuss a smoothie recipe for a character from a Roald Dahl book, for example Violet Beauregarde from Charlie and the Chocolate Factory. How can an existing recipe be adapted to reflect that character? Or can children write a recipe for a brand new smoothie? Children plan: • what will be needed (ingredients and equipment) • what will need to be done (in order). Repeat the process for a hot soup based on a Roald Dahl character. **Designing** Children write or adapt a recipe for either a cold smoothie or a hot soup based on their favourite character. (Use the 'Cooking: designing and making sheet' from the CD-ROM.) Make sure there is time to discuss the recipes and alter them if necessary.
Making	• To prepare ingredients by cutting and shaping using appropriate tools. • To work safely and hygienically. • To measure and weigh ingredients accurately. • To prepare and cook food using a heat source. • To decorate food appropriately to ensure a good finish.	Before beginning to make soup or smoothie, remind children about basic hygiene and safety procedures. In groups children create a poster of the dos and don'ts of food hygiene and safety, providing images to act as prompts/stimuli. Children follow their completed 'Cooking: designing and making sheets' to create their smoothie or soup product. **Technical knowledge** Teach children to assemble all of their ingredients and cooking utensils before they start. Remind children of the correct procedures for cutting and preparing a range of fruit and vegetables to be used in their recipes. Children preparing hot soup should be supervised at all times when using a heat source.
Evaluating	• To use an increasing vocabulary to describe the taste, smell, texture and feel of food. • To express a preference about the likes and dislikes of their finished product. • To list the ways in which the finished product meets the design criteria.	**Evaluating their own ideas and products** **Discussion: What makes a good smoothie or soup?** Children decide on five criteria to judge each product (these could be the five criteria used on the 'Cooking: evaluation sheet'). Working in small groups, children taste and evaluate each other's smoothies or soups using the evaluation sheet. Display a word bank for children to use to describe the smoothie or soup: smooth, lumpy, sweet, bitter, sharp, gritty, thick, runny, etc. **Extension**: Challenge children to design soups and smoothies for other favourite book characters.

Notes:
Roald Dahl's Completely Revolting Recipes (Red Fox), provides lots of interesting recipes. Children could organise a Roald Dahl character party where they prepare some of the recipes made in this unit (and in the book) and wear their party hats made in the associated unit.

Cross-curricular links:
English: children's stories written by Roald Dahl; links with non-fiction writing – instructional texts

Year 3 Medium-term planning: 1B Roald Dahl: Party hats

Design brief: To design and make a party hat to wear to a Roald Dahl character party.

P	Learning objectives	Creative, technical and practical activities
Designing	• To investigate similar products to get ideas and to use as a starting point for an original design. • To develop more than one design or adapt an initial design to produce a final design. • To use a computer to help in designing or modelling ideas. • To choose appropriate sheet materials that are fit for purpose.	Introduce the design brief and following a discussion, children choose a favourite character from a story written by Roald Dahl. **Generating, developing, modelling and communicating ideas** Children create a 'scrap page' about their character. From researching the internet and from the actual books, they add copies of drawings/ photographs/stills from movies to the 'scrap page' and also add descriptive dialogue from the actual book. (Model how to create a 'scrap page' as a shared lesson with the class based on a Roald Dahl or other character.) The 'scrap page' will act as the main stimulus for the design of the hat. **Focused practical task (FPT)** Show children how to create the basic hat design (thick card around the base with a strap crossing the top of the head). Working in pairs, children help each other to create a basic hat that fits each of them, as a starting point for their own hat design. **Designing** Children draw the basic hat design and then using their 'scrap page' they add additional features, decorations and shapes, to create a hat reflecting their chosen character. They can then add colour to their design. Give children a list of art materials they can use to add colour, decoration and character to their hat, for example, paint, feathers, coloured paper, sequins, ribbons, jewels, etc. Encourage them to label their design to show what materials they used.
Making	• To cut accurately and safely following lines and markings. • To cut internal shapes and designs in sheet materials. • To cut slots to join sheet materials together. • To join and combine materials. • To apply a range of decorative finishing techniques.	**Practical skills and techniques** Demonstrate how to create a card template of the additional features for the hat. Children then create their own template, based on their design. This is cut out and then decorated before attaching to the basic hat design. **Technical knowledge** Demonstrate a range of ways of joining two pieces of card together using: • glue • staples • slots • sticky tape / masking tape. When assembling their hats, children decide on the best method to join the card pieces.
Evaluating	• To express a preference about the likes and dislikes of their finished product. • To consider and list ways in which their design or product could be improved. • To list the ways in which the finished product meets the design criteria. • To discuss the effectiveness of the method and techniques used in making the product.	**Evaluating their own ideas and products** Children work in pairs to evaluate their party hats. They could use the following questions as a basis for their evaluations: • Do I like my party hat? Do I like my friend's party hat? • What are its good features? • What could be better? • Does it remind me of a Roald Dahl story character? • How strong is it? • Did I/they use the right methods to join the pieces? Give children copies of the 'Product evaluation sheet' from the CD-ROM to record their findings.

Notes:
It would be useful if the teacher models every phase in the design and make process by creating a hat based on a Roald Dahl character. Children could organise a Roald Dahl character party at which they wear their party hat and eat some of the food made in the associated unit.

Cross-curricular links:
Literacy links: children's stories written by Roald Dahl

Year 3 Medium-term planning: 2A Kings and Queens:
Fit for a king or queen

Design brief: To design and make bread rolls for a royal breakfast.

P	Learning objectives	Creative, technical and practical activities
Designing	• To know the types of food that are grown. • To know that food is processed into ingredients for cooking. • To use an increasing vocabulary to describe the taste, smell, texture and feel of food. • To know that a recipe can be adapted to change the taste, appearance and smell. • To follow a recipe. • To work safely and hygienically.	**Generating, developing, modelling and communicating ideas** Discuss bread and its importance as part of a healthy diet. *How many different ways is bread eaten?* (rolls, toast, naan bread, sandwiches, pizza, etc.) *What types of bread are there?* (white, brown, wholemeal, etc.) **Evaluating existing products (EEP): Bread** Evaluate five different bread products for taste, texture, smell, appearance and shape. (These are the five criteria used in the 'Cooking evaluation sheet'.) **Focused practical task (FPT)** Children should follow a basic bread recipe. They mix and knead the dough and then allow it to prove before baking. **Technical knowledge** Teach children that flour is a processed food that is milled from grains such as wheat. They should know that the type of flour used will affect the flavour of the bread and the type of liquid used will affect the texture. Teach children the role of yeast in bread making. In groups, children make a basic bread recipe that is shaped into small rolls. Introduce children to the design brief, explain that in designing and making their breakfast roll (the product), they are allowed to: • add one additional ingredient • create their own shape for a bread roll. **Discussion: What would be a good additional ingredient for a royal breakfast roll?** As a class make a list of additional ingredient suggestions (chocolate drops, jam, honey etc.) always giving reasons for why they would add them. **Discussion: What would be a good shape for a royal breakfast roll?** Children experiment with play dough or salt dough they have made themselves to create different shapes for a bread roll – twisting, curling, shaping, and plaiting. This can be accompanied by research on the internet for different bread roll shapes. Children create a simple design sheet on which they draw the shape of their roll, list the added ingredient and describe how and when the extra ingredient will be added.
Making	• To prepare and combine ingredients using a range of techniques and appropriate tools. • To measure and weigh ingredients accurately. • To prepare and cook food using a heat source. • To decorate food appropriately to ensure a good finish.	In groups of five, children make the basic bread recipe which is proved and then divided equally between the group members. Following their design sheet, children create their own product by adding the additional ingredient and then shaping their rolls. Remind children to assemble or their ingredients and cooking utensils before they start and that there are basic hygiene and safety procedures to follow.
Evaluating	• To use an increasing vocabulary to describe the taste, smell, texture and feel of food. • To express a preference about the likes and dislikes of their finished product.	**Evaluating their own ideas and products** Children repeat the evaluation exercise from the making phase (using the 'Cooking: evaluation sheet' from the CD-ROM) this time using their own bread roll product. Give time for children to reflect on the whole process: • What did you enjoy doing? • Would you make bread again? • What would you change or adapt?

Notes:
When making a basic bread recipe, the lessons need to be timed so that the dough has sufficient time to prove.
Visit www.scholastic.co.uk/100designandtechnology for a 'How to make bread' activity sheet.

Cross-curricular links:
History: British Kings and Queens, royal dynasties from other nations or cultures

Year 3 Medium-term planning: 2B Kings and Queens: Royal photo frame

Design brief: To design and make a photo frame to sell at the Buckingham Palace shop.

P	Learning objectives	Creative, technical and practical activities
Designing	• To investigate similar products and list their key features. • To draw, photograph and label products to show an understanding of how they are made or how they work. • To plan a sequence of actions to make a product. • To use labelled drawings and notes to explain how their product will be made.	**Evaluating existing products (EEP): Photo frames** Provide a collection of photo frames for children to evaluate. When evaluating photo frames encourage children to: • handle, discuss and draw different free-standing photo frames • identify how the photograph is protected using Perspex/glass • identify how the photograph frame stands up • choose one photo frame that they photograph and then label, identifying: the different parts of the frame, the materials it is made from, how it is decorated and the method of support. Children undertake a practical investigation to make an A5 sheet of thick card stand up on its own. They consider how to make the structure stable by using an additional piece of card/triangulation, etc. Give children the opportunity to examine images of the British crown jewels and list the common features associated with them (metals used, jewels, fur/ermine). Which of these elements do they want to include in their design? **Designing** Children use the 'My design' sheet from the CD-ROM to design their royal photo frames. They should include: • how the frame will stand upright • the method of fixing the photograph in place and protecting the photograph • materials to construct the frame (thick cardboard) • how to decorate the frame to reflect the design criteria. As part of the design process (included on the 'My design sheet') children create an action plan to follow when making their product.
Making	• To choose appropriate sheet materials that are fit for purpose. • To cut accurately and safely following lines and markings. • To cut internal shapes and designs in sheet materials. • To join and combine materials using glue to fix them together. • To apply a range of decorative finishing techniques.	**Technical knowledge** Demonstrate how to cut accurately using a craft knife and sharp scissors, including cutting an internal shape to create the frame. **Practical skills and techniques** • Children collect together all the materials and tools that they will need. • They identify tasks that they may need help with (using a craft knife and/or glue gun). • They follow their action plans.
Evaluating	• To express a preference about the likes and dislikes of their finished product. • To consider and list ways in which their design or product could be improved. • To discuss the effectiveness of the materials used in making the product.	**Evaluating their own ideas and products** When evaluating their finished photo frame, children can use the 'Product evaluation sheet' from the CD-ROM to list: • what they liked/disliked about their design • which of the materials they used worked well/didn't work well • two or three ways in which they could improve their design. **Role play** Children dress up as kings and queens and have their photograph taken for the photo frames. They could then be filmed giving their opinions about different photo frames. **Extension**: Challenge children to modify their photo frame design for a different royal family from another culture: ancient Egypt, ancient China etc.

Notes:
Children should have the opportunity to handle and look at different examples of photo frames.
Health and safety: If possible, avoid using photograph frames with glass fronts.
Digital: This unit could be designed, 'made' and displayed using digital tools.

Cross-curricular links:
History: British royal family, royal dynasties from other nations, cultures or times

Year 3 Medium-term planning: 3A Ancient Egypt: Pop-up book

Design brief: To design and make pages for a pop-up book about ancient Egypt.

P	Learning objectives	Creative, technical and practical activities
Designing	• To investigate similar products to get ideas and to use as a starting point for an original design. • To draw, photograph and label products to show an understanding of how they are made or how they work. • To use technical vocabulary when designing and planning a product.	**Evaluating existing products (EEP): Pop-up books** Give children the opportunity to evaluate a range of pages from pop-up books, first sorting the book pages into those which have 'pop-ups' and those which work by a simple mechanism. Suggest they take digital photographs of the pages then print them out, label them and explain how each mechanism works and how the movement is generated. **Focused practical task (FPT)** Teach children, through focused practical tasks, the following range of pop-up mechanisms: • simple flap/door mechanism • pop-up V-fold • pop-up parallel-fold • fixed pivot lever mechanism • moving pivot level mechanism. After each FPT the children in groups design a book page about ancient Egypt that incorporates the mechanism that they have learned. They should draft out the page indicating how the mechanism will work, where the illustrations will be and the position and content of the text. (It may be useful to give guidance on how to draft the page and then demonstrate how to turn the draft into the finished product.) Children: • should decide on the design criteria that will enable them to produce a quality pop-up book about ancient Egypt (reference back to EEP activity) • will need to assign different roles for each member of the group • can consider opportunities for the text/illustrations to be produced using ICT.
Making	• To cut accurately and safely following lines and markings. • To cut internal shapes and designs in sheet materials. • To create different levers and linkages. • To create and use complex pop-up mechanisms for pages of books. • To join and combine materials using glue to fix them together. • To apply a range of decorative finishing techniques.	Children use their design draft to guide them as they make each page of their pop-up book. They should have access to a range of sheet materials, fixings and colouring pens and pencils to allow them to complete each page. **Technical knowledge** Demonstrate and ensure children are skilled in using: • a hole punch or paper drill • paper fasteners effectively. Listed are some suggestions for how to make each mechanism into a page of a book about ancient Egypt: • simple flap/door mechanism: ancient Egyptian timeline of events • pop-up V-fold: pyramids • pop-up parallel-fold: temples and ancient Egyptian gods • fixed pivot lever mechanism: how the shaduf was used for water collection. As children work on their storybooks, they should be stopped at regular intervals to give them the opportunity to assess how their product is progressing. This also provides opportunities for mini-plenaries to reinforce safety rules and to share examples of good practice.
Evaluating	• To consider and list ways in which their design or product could be improved. • To list the ways in which the finished product meets the design criteria.	**Evaluating their own ideas and products** • As part of the evaluation process, each group should have the opportunity to present their pop-up book pages to the rest of the class. • Each group should evaluate their pop-up book against the agreed design criteria using the 'Product evaluation sheet' from the CD-ROM. • The pop-up books can be loaned to another class to look at for a week and then children could collect feedback and comments about their books.

Notes:
This unit of work builds on the Year 1 unit Celebration time: Pop-up cards.

Cross-curricular links:
History: ancient Egypt
English: non-fiction information books

Year 3 Medium-term planning: 3B Ancient Egypt: Cleopatra's cushion

Design brief: To design and make a cushion, fit for an Egyptian Queen!

P	Learning objectives	Creative, technical and practical activities
Designing	• To investigate similar products to get ideas and to use as a starting point for an original design. • To use labelled drawings and notes to explain how their product will be made.	Children study images of Cleopatra paying particular attention to images of her face and the jewellery she wore. Give children copies of the 'My design' sheet from the CD-ROM. They discuss the images with a peer and make notes. Introduce children to the materials to be used in creating their cushions, including the decorative materials and the embroidery possibilities. Give children time to create their own coloured design of a cushion cover for Cleopatra, first using pencils. Encourage them to change and adapt their drawing as they discuss it, finishing by using felt-tipped pens to complete their design. Children should use labels to identify the different ways in which they will decorate their design. This allows them to make a list of the materials and equipment they will need to create their cushion cover. The majority of the design will be created using fabric paint and pens. In addition, provide a range of additional decorative materials, such as ribbons, braids, buttons, beads, etc. (If possible with gold and silver the predominant colours.) In addition, allow children to use embroidery stitches to decorate their cushion. (This could form the basis of an additional FPT, investigating different decorative stitches and learning how to attach beads, buttons and ribbons. For the decorative stitching children can practise using strips of Binca and a range of decorative cross-stitching.)
Making	• To join fabrics together using a range of different sewing techniques. • To apply a range of decorative techniques to different fabric materials. • To create 3D fabric products by combining pieces and using a seam allowance.	**Focused practical task (FPT)** Children make a simple cushion pad by combining two squares of cotton using a running stitch to create a seam. Three sides are sewn up, filling is then added and then the final side is sewn to complete the cushion. To create the cushion cover, children cut out two identical squares of calico fabric, large enough to cover their cushion, with an allowance for the seam. Then they use their design sheet to: • draw and colour the basic design using fabric pens and paints on to one piece of the calico • add additional decorative finishes • sew the two calico pieces together (with the design facing inwards) to create a cushion cover with a seam allowance and the sewn cushion cover is then turned inside out to reveal the finished design. > **Technical knowledge** > Show children a range of different ways in which to use fastenings to finish off their cushion design from which they choose one: buttons, zip and Velcro strips. Finally the cushion cover is fitted over the cushion pad to complete the product.
Evaluating	• To understand how individuals and companies in design technology have helped shape the world.	For the evaluation phase, discuss the home furnishing industry with children. Give them the opportunity to study catalogues (books or online) of some well-known high street home furnishing companies such as Habitat, IKEA or Alessi. Ask children to identify other types of fabric products that are made for the home, for example: curtains, bed linen and towels. **Extension**: Design other fabric items based on the Cleopatra theme or a theme of their own choosing, such as a: pencil case, school bag or mobile phone cover.

Notes:
Reference material relating to Cleopatra's Needle is available on the Scholastic web site (www.scholastic.co.uk/100designandtechnology).
Information about Habitat, IKEA or Alessi and their designers can be obtained from the Design Museum archive or online.

Cross-curricular links:
History: ancient Egypt

Year 3 Background knowledge

Roald Dahl: Swampy, soupy, smoothies

Whilst teaching this unit of work, the emphasis should be on encouraging children to eat at least five portions of fruit and vegetables every day. Almost all fruit and vegetables count towards '5-a-day'. Vegetables, fresh fruit, tinned fruit, dried fruit or fruit juice all count.

There is no limit to how much fruit and vegetables can be consumed – so the more you eat, the better. Children should be taught to eat a variety of fruit and vegetables to get the maximum nutritional benefits. This is because fruit and vegetables contain different combinations of fibre, vitamins, minerals and other nutrients.

Video resources:
BBC Learning Website – Design Technology Videos: *The importance of handwashing in food hygiene* and *Five types of food*.

Roald Dahl: Party hats

Website recommendation: www.roalddahl.com

Kings and Queens: Fit for a king or queen

Video resources: BBC Learning Website – Design Technology Video: The bread-making process and Does eating breakfast affect concentration?

Kings and Queens: Royal photo frame

Website recommendation: www.royalcollectionshop.co.uk

Ancient Egypt: Pop-up book

www.scholastic.co.uk online shop has a range of downloadable materials that feature pop-up books and mechanisms.

The following websites offer extensive explanations and/or further links about pop up mechanisms:
www.popupbooks.com (explanations and PDFs to download and make)
www.childrensengineering.com/linkspopups.htm
www.mr-d-n-t.co.uk (excellent site with links to YouTube video demonstrations)

Ancient Egypt: Cleopatra's cushion

Video resources: BBC Learning Website – Design Technology Videos: *Design and make your own cushion covers* and *Sewing a mobile phone cover*

Children can experiment with and develop different decorative sewing techniques using Binca sheets. They should develop derivatives of both the diagonal cross-stitch and also vertical and horizontal stitches and create different patterns by using different colours and leaving gaps in their stitches.

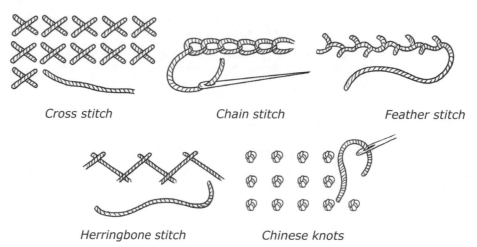

Cross stitch   Chain stitch   Feather stitch

Herringbone stitch   Chinese knots

Year 4 Long-term planning

Design

The National Curriculum states that when designing and making, children should be taught to:
- use research and develop design criteria to inform the design of innovative, functional, appealing products that are fit for purpose, aimed at particular individuals or groups
- generate, develop, model and communicate their ideas through discussion, annotated sketches, cross-sectional and exploded diagrams, prototypes, pattern pieces and computer-aided design.

Research a range of areas to inform their designing and making process, including:
- yoghurt and pizzas
- modern abstract art
- wallets and purses
- analogue clocks.
- lamps and lights

Model and communicate their ideas through:
- drawings, illustrations and photographs
- using a standardised design sheet to convey their ideas
- labelled diagrams and diagrams with annotations
- illustrated action plans and flow charts
- formal letters.

Make

The National Curriculum states that when designing and making, children should be taught to:
- select from and use a wider range of tools and equipment to perform practical tasks (for example, cutting, shaping, joining and finishing), accurately
- select from and use a wider range of materials and components, including construction materials, textiles and ingredients, according to their functional properties and aesthetic qualities.

Use a range of tools across each area of design technology, including:
- utensils to cut and prepare food ingredients
- sewing equipment
- scissors and card snips
- saw
- PVA glue.

Use a range of materials to make their products, including:
- paper, card and cardboard
- fabric materials
- sheet materials
- simple electrical components
- wood strips.

Evaluate

The National Curriculum states that when designing and making, children should be taught to:
- investigate and analyse a range of existing products
- evaluate their ideas and products against their own design criteria and consider the views of others to improve their work
- understand how key events and individuals in design and technology have helped shape the world.

Investigate and evaluate a range of products including:
- yoghurts and pizzas
- nightlights
- food packaging
- a magical box.
- Roman-style purses

Gain an understanding of how design and technology have shaped the world in which we live through:
- Understanding what is meant by the term 'convenience food' and researching where food dishes originate from.

Technical knowledge

The National Curriculum states that when designing and making, children should be taught to:
- apply their understanding of how to strengthen, stiffen and reinforce more complex structures
- understand and use mechanical systems in their products (for example, gears, pulleys, cams, levers and linkages)
- understand and use electrical systems in their products (for example, series circuits incorporating switches, bulbs, buzzers and motors)
- apply their understanding of computing to program, monitor and control their products.

Develop and consolidate technical knowledge in the following areas:
- creating wooden frames that are strengthened using triangular struts
- making simple circuits to make a bulb light using a switch.

Cooking and nutrition

The National Curriculum states that children should be taught to:
- understand and apply the principles of a healthy and varied diet
- prepare and cook a variety of predominantly savoury dishes using a range of cooking techniques
- understand seasonality, and know where/how a variety of ingredients are grown, reared, caught and processed.

Develop and consolidate their knowledge and understanding of healthy eating and nutrition by:
- making a batch of yoghurt from milk and live yoghurt
- preparing and adding ingredients to yoghurt
- making pizza bases, tomato sauce and a range of pizza toppings.

Overview of progression in Year 4

Designing

Throughout units of work in Year 4 children:

- investigate similar products to get ideas, list key features and understand how they work
- describe the purpose of their products
- explain how parts and whole of products work and how they will be made
- research information about the needs and wants of users
- develop design criteria to inform ideas
- use prototypes and pattern pieces
- make design decisions taking account of the availability of resources.

Making and technical knowledge: Cooking and nutrition

By designing and making a yoghurt using Ancient Greek ingredients and through pizza art, children:

- select suitable tools and equipment and materials and components and explain choice
- list the order of the main stages of making and produce lists of required tools, equipment and materials
- know how to prepare and cook a variety of predominantly savoury dishes safely and hygienically including the use of a heat source
- know how food is processed into ingredients that can be eaten or used in cooking
- know how to use a range of techniques such as peeling, chopping, slicing, grating and mixing
- assemble and measure ingredients accurately to make recipes
- understand that recipes can be adapted to change appearance, taste, texture and aroma
- use technical vocabulary correctly and with increasing regularity to describe taste, smell, texture and feel of food
- understand that ingredients can be fresh, pre-cooked and processed and that a recipe can be adapted by adding or substituting ingredients.

Making and technical knowledge: Textiles

By designing and making a Roman-style drawstring purse, children:

- select suitable tools and equipment and materials and components
- explain choice of tools and equipment depending on skills and techniques to be used
- measure, mark out, cut and shape textile materials with increasing accuracy
- assemble, join and combine textile materials with increasing accuracy
- apply a range of finishing techniques, with increasing accuracy
- understand that materials can be combined and mixed to create more useful characteristics
- use technical vocabulary correctly and with increasing regularity to describe sewing techniques and fabrics
- know that a single fabric shape can be used to make a 3D textiles product.

Year 4 Complete 'Overview of progression' is provided on the CD-ROM, including 'Making and technical knowledge: Construction', 'Making and technical knowledge: Sheet materials' and 'Evaluating' objectives.

Year 4 Medium-term planning: 1A Ancient times: Greek yoghurt

Design brief: To design and make a yoghurt using traditional ancient Greek ingredients.

P	Learning objectives	Creative, technical and practical activities
Designing	• To investigate similar products to get ideas and to use as a starting point for an original design. • To investigate similar products and list their key features. • To plan a sequence of actions to make a product. • To know that dairy produce comes from animal milk. • To know that food is processed into ingredients for cooking. • To analyse and state a preference about the taste, smell, texture and the look of food.	**Evaluating existing products (EEP): Yogurt** **Discussion**: *Where does yoghurt come from? How is it made? Who has eaten yoghurt before? What kind is your favourite?* Children should be able to identify which part of 'The eatwell plate' yoghurt belongs to. Conduct a 'yoghurt tasting' session by blind-tasting five different strawberry yoghurts, giving each a mark out of ten. Investigate whether the most expensive yoghurt is in fact always the tastiest. They record their findings on the 'Cooking: evaluation sheet'. Investigate types of food from ancient Greece which would be suitable to use in yoghurt, using an internet search. Children should have the opportunity to taste some traditional ingredients such as, honey, figs, grapes, pomegranates and pine nuts. Discuss food packaging and ask: *What information is contained on yoghurt packaging and is it common to all food packaging?* **Designing** As a class, children decide on a list of food eaten in ancient Greece that would be suitable to use in a yoghurt.
Making	• To create plans that can be used by someone else to make the product. • To write a recipe. • To know that a recipe can be adapted to change the taste, appearance and smell. • To prepare ingredients by cutting and shaping using appropriate tools. • To work safely and hygienically. • To prepare and cook food using a heat source.	**Focused practical task (FPT): Making yogurt from milk using live yoghurt** Demonstrate how to make yoghurt using milk and fresh, live, yoghurt (see background notes), explaining how yoghurt is formed by bacteria fermenting the milk. Children repeat the task experimenting with different types of milk, to see whether different types of milk affect the taste and texture. They try: • full fat cow's milk • skimmed milk • semi-skimmed milk • soya or almond milk • goat's milk • flavoured milk (strawberry, banana). They carry out a yoghurt 'tasting session' to gather results of the experiment. Children design and make their own Greek yoghurt, making decisions about: • type of milk they will use • ingredients that they will add to the yoghurt • any ingredient preparation needed, for example, finely chopping, making a puree, etc. They make their yoghurt and then write a recipe using ICT, giving ingredients and exact instructions on how to make an ancient Greek yoghurt. Children design a label for their ancient Greek yoghurt by combining pictures and text, including a list of ingredients. If using desktop publishing software, the design can be printed on to a sticky label and stuck to a plain yoghurt pot to create a 'mock up' yoghurt pot.
Evaluating	• To express a preference about the likes and dislikes of their finished product and of similar products produced in the class.	**Evaluating their own ideas and products** • Children evaluate each other's yoghurt recipes in a 'blind taste test'. • They give each yoghurt marks 'out of ten' and the most popular is declared the winner. • Children should also have the opportunity to evaluate the yoghurt pot design.

Notes:
Check food allergy requirements of all children before undertaking the testing and tasting of yoghurts.

Year 4 Medium-term planning: 1B Ancient times: Roman purse

Design brief: To design and make a 'Roman-style' drawstring money purse.

P	Learning objectives	Creative, technical and practical activities
Designing	• To investigate similar products to get ideas and to use as a starting point for an original design. • To draw, photograph and label products to show an understanding of how they are made or how they work. • To use technical vocabulary when designing and planning to make a product.	**Evaluating existing products (EEP): Wallets and purses** Provide a range of different wallets and purses for children to examine and which they then express a preference, and reasons for their choices. Children choose one wallet/purse to examine more closely. They draw a detailed labelled diagram of the purse, including notes on the types of materials used, types of fastenings and the decoration that has been applied. **Focused practical task (FPT)** Following clear instructions, children make their own Roman 'bulla' purse from circular cloth and using a running stitch to create the drawstring. Encourage children to discuss the differences between this design and the modern purses they have been evaluating. Give children the opportunity to study a range of images of Roman purses to note the style. There could be an option to design and make a more elaborate version of the 'bulla' or to design a drawstring purse; this involves cutting and stitching together pieces of felt. Whichever option is chosen, show children how to create a stitched hem in which the drawstring is enclosed – an improvement on the bulla design. **Focused practical task (FPT): Creating a hem in the material for the drawstring** Show children how to make a hem in some material. Children draw their design, including labels, notes and in particular, how they will decorate their purse using stitching in a 'Roman' style. They also list the stages in which they will make their design.
Making	• To join fabrics together using a range of different sewing techniques. • To use a range of fastenings. • To cut a range of fabrics accurately using a pattern. • To apply a range of decorative techniques to different fabric materials.	Using the 'My design sheet' as a guide, children should first practise their decorative stitching techniques on a felt sample. This sampler is then attached to their design sheet for later reference. Children work through the stages on their design sheet to make their purse.
Evaluating	• To express a preference about the likes and dislikes of their finished product. • To consider and list ways in which their design or product could be improved. • To list the ways in which the finished product meets the design criteria.	**Evaluating their own ideas and products** Children write a report about their Roman-style purses. In writing their report they evaluate their finished product answering questions, such as: • What were the design criteria for the purse? Who was the purse designed for? • How successful is the purse in keeping money secured, and how do you know? • How did using images of Roman purses help in your design? • Which features of your decoration are Roman in style? • How happy are you with your finished product? • How could you improve your design work next time? • How has the design of purses changed since Roman times?

Notes:
As an extension to this activity, children could design and make some amulets or lucky charms from clay that are sprayed gold or silver and are displayed alongside their finished products.

Cross-curricular links:
Art and design activities, depending on school plan.

Year 4 Medium-term planning: 2A Magic: A magical light

Design brief: To design and make a magical night light for someone who is afraid of the dark!

P	Learning objectives	Creative, technical and practical activities
Designing	• To investigate similar products for ideas and to use as a starting point for an original design. • To use labelled drawings and notes to explain how their product will work. • To create an action plan using pictures or a flow diagram. • To use technical vocabulary when designing and planning to make a product.	**Generating, developing, modelling and communicating ideas** Display and discuss a range of images of lights in different contexts, for example, in the home, at school, in the local community, including if possible some unusual and distinctive examples. Discuss what each light is used for and how it works. • How is the design of each light suited to its uses? • How does it work – what type of electricity? (batteries or mains) • How is it switched on or off? **Evaluating existing products (EEP): Light sources** Lead an investigation, carefully taking apart a light source to see how it is made, for example, a torch, bike lamp, table lamp. Explain how the light works and identify key features: bulb, reflector, battery, switch and casing. Explain how the casing is designed to keep the user safe and that certain parts of the light act as insulators. Especially focus on the electrical circuit and how a complete circuit is made using a switch. **Focused practical task (FPT)** Challenge children to create their own simple circuit using a battery, bulb, a switch and connecting wires (see background knowledge). Drawing the circuit that they have made (extension: using proper circuit diagram components), they including labels to show their understanding of how it works. Demonstrate how a reflector can be used to direct light in certain directions. Provide a range of materials with reflective qualities. Children experiment with how to incorporate them into their simple circuit to direct the light in one direction. Introduce the task of designing a nightlight. • Show images and designs – what are the most popular designs? Why? • What is the function of a nightlight? (ambient, not direct light) Agree, through discussion, what their design should include, for example: • paper shade/casing • simple light circuit • a switch that is suitable for the product • reflector • cardboard or wooden base. Children produce a labelled diagram that shows the above features, how the circuit will work and the materials and tools that will be needed. (Give children copies of the 'My design sheet' to support them with this task.)
Making	• To use a simple circuit in a model with a bulb or buzzer. • To create a frame structure with diagonal struts for added strength. • To cut internal shapes and designs in sheet materials. • To apply a range of decorative finishing techniques.	Provide materials for children to select and construct their nightlight, incorporating the circuit and switches as per their design. **Technical knowledge** Check that children understand the role of all components in the circuit.
Evaluating	• To list the ways in which the finished product meets the design criteria.	**Evaluating their own ideas and products** Display, and if possible, use the nightlights then evaluate them using questions, such as: • Does your nightlight work? • Does it switch on and off easily? • Does the base provide a stable structure for the light? • What would you improve about your nightlight? • Which nightlight do you like the most? Why?

Notes:
Health and safety: stress to the children that they are never to take apart any electrical equipment, and discuss the dangers of mains electricity and the importance of electricity in our lives.

Cross-curricular links:
Science: electricity and simple circuits

Year 4 Medium-term planning: 2B Magic: The magic box

Design brief: To design and make a magic box based on the poem by Kit Wright.

P	Learning objectives	Creative, technical and practical activities
Designing	• To develop more than one design or adapt an initial design to produce a final design.	Introduce children to the poem 'The Magic Box' by Kit Wright. Give them time to analyse the poem and to list the different things that are being put into the box. **Designing** Children use the poem as a stimulus to draw five 'picture scenes' of the items that are placed into the magic box or they write their own version of the poem which they then use to draw the five 'picture scenes'. (These five scenes will form the decoration for the four sides and the lid of the magic box they are going to make.)
Making	• To create a frame structure with diagonal struts for added strength. • To create stable frames using a range of materials. • To cut wood using a range of tools accurately. • To use a glue gun safely. • To join materials appropriately using a range of techniques. • To cut accurately and safely following lines and markings. • To join and combine materials using glue to fix them together. • To apply a range of decorative finishing techniques.	**Technical knowledge** Teach children to make a square wood frame using 10mm square section wood (15cm x 15cm) that is strengthened using thick card triangles to make a rigid structure. This will from part of their box frame. Lynx corner joints are used with the card triangles to ensure the corners are at right angles and a quality finish. **Focused practical task (FPT)** Once the square wood frame has been successfully completed, children are challenged to create a cube, making an identical square frame and joining both together with additional wood lengths of 10cm x 10cm. Then an additional frame (10cm x 10cm) is constructed for the lid of the box. Children create the sides, the lid and bottom of the box from card that they decorate according to their design. When completed the card can be laminated to provide additional strength and a better quality finish. The card sides are cut to size and added to the frame to complete the magic box. Children investigate ways of making a hinge joint using different materials and also a fastening for the box using ribbon, Velcro, etc. Also, children may want to create a lining for their box by attaching material to the inside.
Evaluating	• To consider and list ways in which their design or product could be improved.	**Evaluating own ideas and products** The question 'How can I make my box more 'magical'?' provides the opportunity for children to evaluate the quality finish of their box. Particularly focusing on: • the accuracy of the measurement and cutting of the wood (this can be done before the sides are added) • the finish where the sides of card meet (are they able to improve this finish using coloured masking tape?) • using additional decorative items such as bows, ribbons, glitter, etc. to embellish the finished design. Extension: There is an opportunity for children to be creative in developing ways to make the box more magical. They can draw a 3D image of the box and label and annotate ways to make it more 'magical'. For example: • playing music when it opens • having a magical locking device. Some children may need help to draw the box in 3D.

Notes:
Although this unit of work is based on the poem 'The Magic Box' by Kit Wright it can easily be adapted for children to create their own treasure box or jewellery box.

Cross-curricular links:
English: 'The Magic Box' and other poetry by Kit Wright

Year 4 Medium-term planning: 3A Piece of art: Pizza art

Design brief: To design and make an abstract art pizza for sale at the Tate Modern cafeteria.

P	Learning objectives	Creative, technical and practical activities
Designing	• To investigate similar products to get ideas and to use as a starting point for an original design. • To use an increasing vocabulary to describe the taste, smell, texture and feel of food. • To analyse and state a preference about the taste, smell, texture and the look of food. • To use labelled drawings and notes to explain how their product will be made. • To create an action plan using pictures or a flow diagram. • To create plans that can be used by someone else to make the product.	**Evaluating existing products (EEP): Pizza** Give children the opportunity to taste a variety of pizzas. Ask them to express a preference for their favourite, by taste and appearance and challenge them to list the different toppings/ingredients in each pizza using the 'Cooking: evaluation sheet'. from the CD-ROM Following a class discussion of the results, children should be able to identify the key common ingredients in pizza and identify which part of 'The eatwell plate' pizza belongs to. **Designing** Give children a range of examples of famous abstract art, or ask them to research examples online, and choose one example to turn into a pizza. Children produce an illustrated and annotated design sheet. Guide them to consider: • the shape, size and thickness of the pizza • how to use the range of ingredients to represent the abstract work of art. As part of the design process, children produce a flow chart for making the pizza. Limit the range of ingredients and give each ingredient a cost, allowing the children to work out the total price of producing their pizza.
Making	• To know that food is processed into ingredients for cooking. • To follow a recipe and know that a recipe can be adapted to change the taste, appearance and smell. • To prepare ingredients by cutting and shaping using appropriate tools. • To work safely and hygienically. • To prepare and cook food using a heat source.	**Focused practical tasks (FPT)** Challenge children to: • make a pizza base • make a tomato base • cut and prepare a range of vegetable, dairy and meat toppings. Using their experience of the FPTs, and having checked their design sheet, children gather all their ingredients and equipment needed and produce their pizza within an agreed timescale. Ask children to write a script for a short video in which they demonstrate how to make the pizza base or the tomato base.
Evaluating	• To list the ways in which the finished product meets the design criteria. • To discuss the effectiveness of the method and techniques used in making the product. • To understand how individuals and companies in design technology have helped shape the world.	**Evaluation** • Children write to the local art gallery explaining about their pizza creation and how it was made, enclosing a photograph. • Pizzas are served to adults in the school (alongside an image of the abstract art); they are asked to comment upon taste and appearance. • Peer assessment – children evaluate each other's flow diagrams to see whether they could have prepared the pizza following the instructions. As part of the evaluation process, talk about where pizza originated and how it has become popular in the UK over the past 30 years. Display photographs or packages of a range of convenience dishes usually found in supermarkets and challenge children to research from which country each dish originates.

Notes:
The title of this unit of work can be changed to the name of a local art gallery.
Care should be taken with the 'taste test' particularly with regard to vegetarians and religious observance.
Visit the Scholastic web site (www.scholastic.co.uk/100designandtechnology) for a step-by-step 'Make a pizza' recipe.

Cross-curricular links:
Art and design: abstract art

Year 4 Medium-term planning: 3B Piece of art: Timeless art

Design brief: To design and make an abstract art clock to sell in the Tate Modern gift shop.

P	Learning objectives	Creative, technical and practical activities
Designing	• To investigate similar products and list their key features. • To draw, photograph and label products to show an understanding of how they are made or how they work. • To create an action plan using pictures or a flow diagram. • To develop more than one design or adapt an initial design to produce a final design.	**Generating, developing, modelling and communicating ideas** • What are the features of a good clock? • What is the primary role of a clock? • How can the design affect its primary role? **Technical knowledge** Show children the inside of an analogue clock or video/animation of how the gears/cogs work and how they turn the hour, minutes and second hands. They can use construction kits that use gears/cogs to experiment in order to help their understanding of how analogue clocks work. **Designing** Introduce the design brief. Children use the internet to research and print out pictures of different clocks, pasting them around the edges of an A3 sheet of paper. Look for and record the common features of these clocks. Show children a limited range of abstract art (see background knowledge). They choose one piece of art to turn into a clock and paste an image of that art work on to their design sheet. Children try out designs for their clock. Encourage them to try out a range of drawn designs before settling on a final design. They draw their final design in the centre of their sheet. Suggest they consider: • size and shape of the clock face • style and colour of the numbers • materials they will use • methods of decoration and finishing to suit their abstract image. Encourage children to label and add notes to their design sheet to show the different features of the clock. From the design sheet the children create an action plan with pictures that detail how they will make the clock and the materials and tools that they will need.
Making	• To choose appropriate sheet materials that are fit for purpose. • To cut accurately and safely following lines and markings. • To cut internal shapes and designs in sheet materials. • To join and combine materials using glue to fix them together. • To apply a range of decorative finishing techniques.	The clock face can be made from thick card or cardboard sheets – children may need to be shown how to use card snips to cut the sheet material. Children use their action plan and the design sheet to make their clock. It is important that the clocks have an actual working mechanism – these are relatively inexpensive from major educational suppliers. Children will require help from an adult to make a hole in the centre of the clock to fit the clock mechanism and to securely adhere the mechanism to the reverse of the clock face using a glue gun.
Evaluating	• To express a preference about the likes and dislikes of their finished product. • To list the ways in which the finished product meets the design criteria. • To understand how key events in design technology have helped shape the world.	**Evaluating their own ideas and products** Agree criteria to use to evaluate their own clock, such as: • Does the clock tell the time accurately? • Is it easy to use the clock to tell the time? • Can you recognise the piece of abstract art it was based on? Children can also evaluate each other's action plans to see whether they could have made the clock following the instructions. The 'Product evaluation sheet' on the CD-ROM could be used for this purpose. This is an opportunity to look at different ways of telling time through history and the effect this has had on civilisations across the world.

Notes:
The title of this unit of work can be changed to the name of a local art gallery.

Cross-curricular links:
Art and design: abstract art

Year 4 Background knowledge

Ancient times: Greek yoghurt

Traditional ancient Greek ingredients suitable for yoghurts are:
apples, oranges, figs, grapes, pears, plums, pomegranates, honey, pine nuts

To make 500ml of yoghurt:
- Heat 500ml of milk in a saucepan to 46°C (the correct temperature is important)
- Remove from heat and add 3 tablespoons of fresh, live, plain yoghurt.
- Pour the mixture into a thermos flask and leave overnight.
- In the morning it will have thickened and turned into yoghurt.

Ancient times: Roman purse

A bulla is a type of necklace with pouch that was worn by ancient Roman children as a protection from evil spirits. The pouch was made of gold, leather, or cloth depending on how wealthy the family was. The inside of a bulla contained amulets or charms. The bulla was presented to a child at birth. A Roman boy would wear the bulla until he became a man and a Roman girl wore the bulla until she got married.

Magic: A magical light

For the focused discussion include images of room lights, table lamp, traffic light, Christmas tree light, nightlight, security light, torch, Hannukah lights and other lights from other religious festivals.

Video resource:
BBC Learning Website – Design Technology
Video: *Batteries and their uses; Circuits, batteries and power sources; Electrical circuits; Dangers of electricity, the adventures of electro mouse; Using circuits to make games and activities*

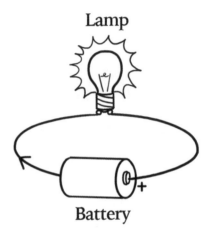

Lamp

Battery

Magic: A magic box

'The Magic Box' by Kit Wright features in many literacy schemes of work and there are many cross-curricular ideas available on the internet.
BBC Learning provides streaming video of the author reading his poetry.

Creating wooden box frames is an important skill to be mastered as these are needed again in units of work in Years 5 and 6.

Video resource: BBC Learning Website – Design Technology Video: *Building a wooden structure*

Piece of art: Pizza art

Suggested examples of abstract art that are suitable for this project:
- *Concentric circles* by Wassily Kandinsky
- Paintings by Piet Mondrian
- *Snail* by Henri Matisse

Ingredients for abstract toppings: cheese squares, sliced peppers, sliced tomatoes, sliced ham, pineapple rings, pepperoni, mushrooms.

Piece of art: Timeless art

Suggested examples of abstract art that are suitable for this project
- *Concentric circles* by Wassily Kandinsky
- Paintings by Piet Mondrian
- *Snail* by Henri Matisse
- Paintings by Joan Miro
- *Le Premier Disque* by Robert Delaunay

Year 5 Long-term planning

Design

The National Curriculum states that when designing and making, children should be taught to:

- use research and develop design criteria to inform the design of innovative, functional, appealing products that are fit for purpose, aimed at particular individuals or groups
- generate, develop, model and communicate their ideas through discussion, annotated sketches, cross-sectional and exploded diagrams, prototypes, pattern pieces and computer-aided design.

Research to inform their designing and making, including: airline meals, flip-flops, cam-based movement toys, Victorian hats, controllable emergency vehicle toy and a working model of a traffic light.

Model and communicate their ideas through:

- drawings, illustrations and photographs
- using a standardised design sheet to convey their ideas, developing more than one idea before deciding on a final design
- constructing a prototype design
- presenting their ideas to a group of people
- creating production method flow diagrams.

Make

The National Curriculum states that when designing and making, children should be taught to:

- select from and use a wider range of tools and equipment to perform practical tasks (for example, cutting, shaping, joining and finishing), accurately
- select from and use a wider range of materials and components, including construction materials, textiles and ingredients, according to their functional properties and aesthetic qualities.

Use a range of tools across each area of design technology, including:

- ICT design software
- scissors and card snips
- saws, hand drills and sandpaper.

Use a range of materials to make their products, including:

- paper, card and cardboard
- wood strips
- acrylic paints and varnish
- fabric materials
- simple electrical components
- sheet materials including bubble wrap and neoprene.

Evaluate

The National Curriculum states that when designing and making, children should be taught to:

- investigate and analyse a range of existing products
- evaluate their ideas and products against their own design criteria and consider the views of others to improve their work
- understand how key events and individuals in design and technology have helped shape the world.

Investigate and evaluate a range of products including:

- commercially produced flip-flops
- mechanical wooden toys
- hats designed in the 21st century
- radio controlled cars.

Gain a better understanding of how design and technology have shaped the world through:

- global food production and its effect on consumers and the environment
- famous hat designers and milliners
- the contribution of traffic lights to road safety.

Technical knowledge

The National Curriculum states that when designing and making, children should be taught to:

- apply their understanding of how to strengthen, stiffen and reinforce more complex structures
- understand and use mechanical systems in their products (for example, gears, pulleys, cams, levers and linkages)
- understand and use electrical systems in their products (for example, series circuits incorporating switches, bulbs, buzzers and motors)
- apply their understanding of computing to program, monitor and control their products.

Develop and consolidate technical knowledge in the following areas:

- creating wooden frames that are strengthened through corner struts
- understanding different cam mechanisms
- creating and using simple circuits that incorporate light, sound and movement.
- using IT software and a control box to control electrical systems from a computer.

Cooking and nutrition

The National Curriculum states that children should be taught to:

- understand and apply the principles of a healthy and varied diet
- prepare and cook a variety of predominantly savoury dishes using a range of cooking techniques
- understand seasonality, and know where/how a variety of ingredients are grown, reared, caught and processed.

Develop and consolidate their knowledge and understanding of healthy eating and nutrition by:

- designing a healthy balanced meal
- understanding that foods are now available all year in the UK due to global food production and improved transportation.

Overview of progression in Year 5

Designing

Throughout units of work in Year 5 children:

- investigate similar products to get ideas, list key features and understand how they work
- research information about the needs and wants of users; later using surveys, interviews, questionnaires and web-based resources
- develop design criteria to inform ideas; later developing a simple design specification as a guide
- explain how parts and whole of products work and how it will be made
- use prototypes and pattern pieces
- use annotated sketches, cross-sectional drawings and exploded diagrams
- make design decisions taking account of the availability of resources and constraints such as time, resources and cost
- use computer-aided design software.

Making: Cooking and nutrition

By designing and making a balanced meal for an airline flight, children:

- know that food is grown, reared, and caught in the UK, Europe and the wider world and that seasons may affect the food available
- know that a healthy diet is made up from a variety and balance of different foods and drinks and that to be active and healthy, food and drink are needed to provide energy for the body
- understand that different foods and drinks contain different substances needed for health: nutrients, water and fibre
- understand that ingredients can be fresh, pre-cooked and processed and that a recipe can be adapted by adding or substituting ingredients.

Making and technical knowledge: Textiles

By designing and making flip-flops for a summer holiday, children:

- select and explain choice of tools and equipment depending on skills and techniques to be used
- select and explain choice of materials and components to fit functional properties and aesthetic qualities
- list the order of the main stages of making and produce lists of required tools, equipment and materials
- measure, mark out, cut and shape textile materials and components with increasing accuracy
- assemble, join and combine materials and components with increasing accuracy
- apply a range of finishing techniques
- understand that materials can be combined and mixed to create more useful characteristics
- use technical vocabulary correctly and with increasing regularity to describe sewing techniques and fabrics.

Year 5 Complete 'Overview of progression' is provided on the CD-ROM, including 'Making and technical knowledge: Construction', 'Making and technical knowledge: Sheet materials' and 'Evaluating' objectives.

Year 5 Medium-term planning: 1A Summer holidays: An airline meal

Design brief: To design and make a balanced meal to serve on a flight.

P	Learning objectives	Creative, technical and practical activities
Designing	• To investigate similar products to get ideas and to use as a starting point for an original design. • To draw, photograph and label products to show an understanding of how they are made or how they work. • To develop more than one design or adapt an initial design to produce a final design.	For this unit, children choose a long-haul holiday destination and design a meal that reflects the cuisine of their destination country. In order to achieve this they need to research: • the typical dishes of that country • what is meant by a 'national dish'. Use the results of the children's search for a classroom display. **Designing** They should also research and/or use their own personal experiences to gather images or designs of an airline meal food tray. In designing their airline meal they need to consider: • what is meant by a healthy balanced diet and to reflect this in their meal design (carbohydrates, protein, water, vegetables, etc.) • what features are typical of a long-haul airline meal (starter, main course, dessert, roll and butter, drinks, cutlery etc.). Children draw how they would present their airline meal on paper to scale, (an airline tray size is 40cm x 30cm) label and annotate the different types of food that will be served, where each will be placed and what else in on the tray. The children could use the 'Cooking: designing and making sheet' from the CD-ROM for this purpose. **Using ICT** • Design name and logo for a catering company making airline meals. • Record relevant information about the country the airline is visiting. • List the food that is to be served. • Explain why the food that they are serving is healthy for the passengers.
Making	• To use a computer to help in designing or modelling ideas. • To understand what is meant by a healthy diet and apply it to product design.	**Making a prototype** Children need a prototype to sell their idea to the airline; part of the design criteria is that the tray and all the plates and utensils must be recyclable. Using their design for an airline meal as a starting point and paper and card, children create a 'mock up' of their airline tray. They create the plates and the food dishes from nets of shapes and use plastic cutlery and cups, etc. It is not necessary for the children to make the actual food. They can collect images of the food they are planning to serve as part of the mock-up.
Evaluating	• To list the ways in which the finished product meets the design criteria. • To discuss the effectiveness of the method and techniques used in making the product. • To understand how individuals, companies and key events in design technology have helped shape the world.	Children present their ideas and prototype as a presentation to the rest of the class. This is a good opportunity to talk about food production. • Where does food come from? Discuss the role of farms in producing animals, cereals, dairy, fruit and vegetables, as opposed to home-grown food production. How many children grow fruit and vegetables, or keep animals for food at home? • Examine a range of produce from the local supermarket. Sort into local produce (sourced from the UK) and produce from outside the UK. Display locations on a map. • Research food grown in the UK and discuss the idea of seasonality of food. Discuss how produce such as tomatoes are now available all year round. Where do tomatoes in the supermarkets come from? Discuss how sourcing food from all over the world is bringing new opportunities to developing countries but that this also has an environmental impact. Research the environmental cost of transporting food.

Notes:

See background knowledge for further information about nutritional advice for children.

Cross-curricular links:

This unit of work links in well with geography topics about different countries or can be linked to study of a specific country. Also discuss what recyclable materials they could use.

Year 5 Medium-term planning: 1B Summer holidays: Flip-flops

Design brief: To design and make a pair of flip-flops for a summer holiday.

P	Learning objectives	Creative, technical and practical activities
Designing	• To investigate similar products to get ideas and to use as a starting point for an original design. • To investigate similar products and list their key features.	**Evaluating existing products (EEP)** Display a collection of flip-flops – actual shoes and images. Discuss the commonality between the shoes. Provide a disassembled example of a flip-flop and discuss its construction, in particular how the strap is fastened to the sole. Discuss the different materials that they are made from (natural or artificial) and how they provide thickness and comfort. From a range of images of commercially sold flip-flops identify common themes: colours, designs, flowers, seaside, pop groups, football teams, etc. Discuss what the key features of a successful flip-flop are: comfort, durability, being waterproof, bright, attractive, etc. Do these influence the design brief for their flip-flop design? **Designing** To design and make a pair of flip-flops for their summer holidays based on a particular theme or style. Children create their design using the 'My design sheet'. Explain to the children that they are making one prototype flip-flop to show to a shoe manufacturer to persuade them to mass produce the design.
Making	• To create prototypes of their product. • To cut a range of fabrics accurately using a pattern. • To use a computer to help in designing or modelling ideas. • To choose appropriate sheet materials that are fit for purpose. • To apply a range of decorative techniques to different materials. • To create 3D fabric products by combining pieces and using a seam allowance. • To join and combine materials using glue to fix them together.	**Focused practical task (FPT)** As the majority of flip-flops follow the same basic design, the making process can be a series of tasks: 1. Making the sole (see background knowledge). This also provides an opportunity for children to experiment with different layers of materials to create the most comfortable flip-flop sole. 2. Creating the decorative design. On a separate paper template the decorative design is drawn and coloured (use of ICT paint or design software would improve the quality of the design). 3. Making the flip-flop (see background knowledge).
Evaluating	• To express a preference about the likes and dislikes of their finished product. • To consider and list ways in which their design or product could be improved. • To list the ways in which the finished product meets the design criteria. • To understand how individuals and companies in design technology have helped shape the world.	Children design a poster (using ICT) and digital images of their finished prototype as part of their sales 'pitch'. They list all the product key points and how it meets the design brief. **Evaluating their own ideas and products** In pairs, children act out the role of a flip-flop manufacturer and designer: • designer showcases all the positive aspects of the flip-flop. • manufacturer suggests ways in which the flip-flop could be improved. This is also an opportunity for children to understand how data collection and analysis is important to manufacturers. Children conduct a shoe size survey in the class and discuss how the results (mode and range) would help a shoe manufacturer to decide how many different sizes and number of shoes to make for the class.

Notes:
Children could research shoe buying and the different types of food sold at different times of the year.

Cross-curricular links:
Art and design: decoration

Year 5 Medium-term planning: 2A A Dickensian Christmas: Mechanical toy

Design brief: To design and make a mechanical toy to take as a gift to a Dickensian Christmas party.

P	Learning objectives	Creative, technical and practical activities
Designing	• To use labelled drawings and notes to explain how their product will be made. • To create an action plan using pictures or a flow diagram. • To create plans that can be used by someone else to make the product. • To use technical vocabulary when designing and planning to make a product. • To construct prototypes and models of products. • To use a cam to make an up and down mechanism. • To understand that different shaped cams produce different movements.	This unit builds upon children's previous work with wheels, axles and different mechanisms. It allows the children to explore cam mechanisms and then use this knowledge when applying it to their own design and making project. **Technical knowledge** Demonstrate how a cam works (there are a number of different cam mechanisms) and show how rotary movement is converted into linear movement. Identify the following parts of the mechanism: cam, cam follower, axle, crank handle. **Evaluating existing products (EEP): Wooden toys** Children have the opportunity to examine and play with a range of wooden toys that use cam mechanisms. They draw one of the toys and label the parts of the cam mechanism, showing on their drawings the direction of rotational movement and linear movement. **Focused practical task (FPT)** Children make a simple cam mechanism using: • a card box (they create themselves using a 3D net) • dowelling for the axle, dowelling and a wheel for the follower • range of different cams. Once completed, investigate further the different linear movements that can be made from changing the cam. They create an annotated set of diagrams to show how different cams affect the way a follower moves. **Designing** Children use the 'My design sheet' from the CD-ROM to design a mechanical toy that uses a cam device. They draw the toy and decide which kind of cam mechanism they will need. Children draw two diagrams – a front view and a back view that shows how the cam mechanism will work (including the different moving parts and direction of movement). Children use the 'My design' sheet to draw an illustrated flow diagram to show the order in which to make the toy.
Making phase	• To create a wooden frame structure with diagonal struts for added strength. • To accurately cut wood using a range of tools accurately.	Children use their design and the illustrated flow diagram to help in the construction of their mechanical toy. When making the toy, children can adapt the cam mechanism that they made as part of the focused practical task. However, with an emphasis on quality and finish of the product, children make a wooden box using a frame structure made of 10mm square wood with sides made of thin strips of wood or balsa wood. Focus on making as much of the toy from wood and creating a quality finish: • ensure smooth finish with sandpaper • use poster or acrylic paint to add colour • varnish to complete the making process.
Evaluating	• To express a preference about the likes and dislikes of their finished product. • To consider and list ways in which their design or product could be improved.	**Evaluating their own ideas and products** • Take a photograph of their finished toy and write a paragraph about how a quality finish was achieved. • Draw a diagram of their finished toy and explain how it works. • Evaluate their toy by giving it a mark out of ten for the quality of the finish (10 = excellent – could not do better, 1 = I think I will start again please). They give reasons for their mark. Children answer the following questions: • Does your cam work? • What changes would you make if you made it again?

Notes:

For the FPT above, many educational suppliers sell whole-class cam sets.

Cross-curricular links:

English: Famous works by the author Charles Dickens (*A Christmas Carol* would be very suitable).

History: Topic on the Victorians and/or the history of toys through time.

Year 5 Medium-term planning: 2B A Dickensian Christmas: A Victorian hat

Design brief: To design and make a Victorian hat to wear to a Dickensian Christmas party.

P	Learning objectives	Creative, technical and practical activities
Designing	• To investigate similar products to get ideas and to use as a starting point for an original design. • To draw, photograph and label products to show an understanding of how they are made or how they work. • To use labelled drawings and notes to explain how their product will be made. • To develop more than one design or adapt an initial design to produce a final design. • To create prototypes of their product.	**Evaluating existing products (EEP): Hats** Children collect a range of images of hats currently being sold today, or provide a collection for them to investigate. For each hat they answer the following questions, and any others they want to add. Children could construct a grid to answer the questions: • Who is the intended user? • What types of materials have been used? • Why have these materials been used? • What do you like about the hat? • What do you dislike about the hat? **Designing** Children then research hats that were worn during the 19th century by either men or women. They collect a range of images to add to a design sheet. Before beginning the final design process for their Victorian hat, children should have the opportunity to experiment with sugar paper and a hand stapler to construct a range of hat prototypes based on Victorian designs. They should focus on: • cutting out the component parts in paper • exploring ways of joining and assembling the component parts. If needed, lead a FPT in which the children are taught how to attach the brim to the main part of the hat by using flaps. When the children are happy with their prototype design, they should finalise their design for the hat. Included in the design should be: • the overall look of the hat • the component pieces of the hat laid out as a template • a method of combining component pieces • a list of materials to be used to cover the hat • a list of additional decorations and embellishments.
Making	• To create a textile pattern. • To cut a range of fabrics accurately using a pattern. • To apply a range of decorative techniques to different fabric materials.	The structure for the hat should be made out of thick card using the template from the design sheet. Children use the same template to cut out fabric material to cover the structure. This material is glued in place. The hat is then decorated according to the children's design sheet. During the making process children are photographed at each stage of working.
Evaluating	• To create an action plan using pictures or a flow diagram. • To create plans that can be used by someone else to make the product. • To express a preference about the likes and dislikes of their finished product. • To understand how individuals and companies in design technology have helped shape the world.	Children use write an illustrated account (using the photographs) of the hat-making process that would act as a guide to someone else making a Victorian hat. Children should have the opportunity to research famous milliners who have designed and made hats over the past hundred years including: Stephen Jones, Philip Treacy and Lilly Dache.

Notes:

Digital: Encourage children to photograph all stages of design, development and making to use in their account or a classroom display.

Visit the Scholastic web site (www.scholastic.co.uk/100designandtechnology) to explore activities on the theme of 'Victorian outfits' and 'Victorian Christmas'.

Cross-curricular links:

History: the Victorians

Year 5 Medium-term planning: 3A On the road: Emergency 999!

Design brief: To design and make a battery powered emergency vehicle.

P	Learning objectives	Creative, technical and practical activities
Designing	• To draw, photograph and label products to show an understanding of how they are made or how they work. • To use labelled drawings and notes to explain how their product will be made. • To develop more than one design or adapt an initial design to produce a final design. • To create plans that can be used by someone else to make the product. • To use technical vocabulary when designing and planning to make a product.	Explain that children are going to design and make a model of an emergency vehicle that is controllable. Ask them to bring in toys from home that are battery operated and controllable. **Evaluating existing products (EEP): Radio controlled cars** From photographs of radio controlled cars, or the real thing, children investigate and identify the key parts, paying particular attention to the method of controlling the car. *How does it function and what does it look like?* Children make detailed labelled diagrams of the toy cars showing how they are made, materials that have been used and how they work. Show children a range of images of emergency vehicles (police, ambulance and fire brigade). *How are they easily identified as emergency vehicles?* (markings, lights, siren sound) **Designing** Children draw some designs for their own model emergency vehicle. Explain that they can make several drawings and that none are a final design, but a series of potential design ideas.
Making	• To create a frame structure with diagonal struts for added strength. • To accurately cut wood using a range of tools accurately. • To attach wheels to a chassis using an axle. • To use a simple circuit in a model with a bulb or buzzer. • To use a simple circuit with a motor and switch in a model. • To draw and create nets of 3D shapes.	**Focused practical task (FPT): Making the vehicle chassis** • Demonstrate how to make a rectangular chassis from 10mm square wood and card triangle corners (reinforce the correct and safe use of tools). • Children create their wooden chassis. • Demonstrate how axles and wheels are added. • Children add either two or three axles. **Focused practical task (FPT): Adding motorised movement, light and sound** • Demonstrate the circuit needed for a motor, buzzer and light (series circuit). • Discuss how a switch could be placed in the circuit and the advantages of doing so. **Designing** Using the chassis and simple circuit information, children finish their design sheet, showing the chassis and body of the vehicle and indicating where the electrical components will be placed. They use labelled drawings and annotation to fully explain their model. Children complete a 3D net for the car body which is cut out, decorated and laminated. They add the car body and electrical circuit equipment to the chassis of the car to complete the model.
Evaluating	• To consider and list ways in which their design or product could be improved.	As part of the evaluation process, children are asked to improve and develop their design by imagining that it was radio controlled. • How would you improve its functions? • What would the radio controller look like and how would it work? Children draw a new design sheet for their emergency vehicle (Mark 2) in which they include a digital photograph of their vehicle and also draw the controller and explain how they would improve it, and how it would work.

Notes:

Chassis building from 10mm wood builds on unit Year 4 Magic: 'The Magic Box' by Kit Wright (wood structures).

This topic can be extended through introducing more elements of control technology by using a control box and control software (see below) to:
• determine the direction of the emergency vehicle
• turn the siren/buzzer on and off
• turn the emergency light on and off or make it flash.

Cross-curricular links:

PSHE: keeping safe and road safety

Year 5 Medium-term planning: 3B On the road:
Traffic lights

Design brief: To design and make a set of traffic lights that are controlled from a computer.

P	Learning objectives	Creative, technical and practical activities

Designing	• To investigate similar products and list their key features.
	• To use labelled drawings and notes to explain how their product will be made.
	• To use labelled drawings and notes to explain how their product will work.
	• To use a computer to help in designing or modelling ideas.
	• To use technical vocabulary when designing and planning to make a product.
		Evaluating existing products (EEP)
		Discussion: *What is the role of traffic lights? Where are the nearest traffic lights to school?*
		
		If possible, children should visit a set of traffic lights and film the sequence, alternately show a short video clip (from YouTube or other video sharing site) to show the sequence of traffic lights.
		
		Provide children with a storyboard with a sequence of outlines of traffic lights. The children record and time the sequence of lights from green to red. Use the storyboard to create a flow diagram to control the lights on a traffic light.
		
		Technical knowledge
		Demonstrate how to use a control box and control software to switch a light on or off.
		Teaching will depend upon whether software is flowchart-based or iconic.
		
		Extension: Children create a short animation clip using scratch or similar computer coding software to demonstrate the sequence of a traffic light.
		
		Designing
		1. Designing the sequence: Using previous experience of flow charts, children design (and test) the sequence to control three lights in a traffic light sequence.
		2. Designing the electrical circuit: Children draw a circuit diagram for the wiring of a traffic light that they will make.
		3. Designing the traffic light: Children design a model of a traffic light from sheet materials, cardboard boxes and cardboard tubes. They should pay particular attention to:
		  • creating a stable base and structure (possibly weighing down the base)
		  • the colour of the structure
		  • how to create different coloured lights: red, amber and green.
		
		The three designs are combined on to one design sheet which the children follow to make the model traffic light.

Making phase	• To use a simple circuit in a model with a bulb. • To create stable frames using a range of materials. • To join materials appropriately using a range of techniques. • To control a model using an ICT control program.	Children understand that there are three stages to the making process: **Stage 1** is to make the electrical circuit and to test the circuit to ensure that it works and follows the correct sequence for a traffic light. **Stage 2** is the creation of the traffic light model: • constructing from sheet materials • ensuring a stable base and rigid structure • checking the quality of the finished product. **Stage 3** is fitting the electrical components into the traffic light model.
Evaluating phase	• To list the ways in which the finished product meets the design criteria. • To discuss the effectiveness of the method and techniques used in making the product. • To understand how key events in design technology have helped shape the world.	Key evaluation for this model is whether it works and also whether the sequence is correct. Investigate whether the model be re-programmed to include a flashing green light before it changes to amber. As an extension activity and to evaluate understanding of this topic, children are challenged to write a flow diagram to control a set of traffic lights at a junction.

Notes:
Children could make a map of the local area, showing all the traffic lights. They time each set and report on the differences.

Cross-curricular links:
ICT: controlling devices using computer software; coding – sequencing a traffic light.
PSHE: road safety

Year 5 Background knowledge

Summer holidays: An airline meal

Children in KS2 should understand that a healthy diet is made up of a variety and balance of different foods as drinks from 'The eatwell plate'. To be active and healthy, food is needed to provide energy for the body. A variety of food is needed in the diet because different foods contain different substances that are needed for health, such as fibre, nutrients and water. Children should learn that foods that are grown are affected by the season and can only be harvested at certain times of the year. Children should know that food is either grown (fruit, vegetables, salads) reared (meat such as pigs, chickens and cattle) or caught (fish) and that different foods are produced in different parts of the UK and the wider world.

Video resource: BBC Learning Website – Design Technology Video: *Five types of food; Eating a varied diet; Food needed by the human body*

Summer holidays: Flip-flops

- Children draw around the sole of their left foot on card, leaving an extra 5mm all the way round, this will form the template.
- The template is used to cut the sole shape from a range of materials (polystyrene foam, bubble wrap, thick foam or neoprene are good materials and this activity could form an additional investigation into which combination provides the best comfort).
- An additional two card templates are used to sandwich the spongy material. The layers are glued together to form the flip-flop sole.
- The 'decorative design' is then glued to the upper side of the sole.
- A hole is made all the way through the sole layers (between the position of the big toe and second toe) – adult help will be required.
- A loop of leather thong or thick shoelace is pushed through the hole and a folded piece of fabric or ribbon is fed through the thong loop to create the strap.
- The thong and fabric are tightened and glued to the sole of the flip-flop.
- An additional card or material template can be added to the base of the sole to tidy it up and create a quality finish.
- Additional decoration may be added to the strap to complete the design.

A Dickensian Christmas: Mechanical toy

Cams are best described as odd-shaped wheels that are used to convert rotary motion into linear motion. As the cam rotates around its axle, the follower follows the shape (cam profile) of the cam. The shape of the cam determines the way in which the follower moves up and down.

Video resource: BBC Learning Website – Design Technology Video: *A collection of mechanical toys*

A Dickensian Christmas: A Victorian hat

Women's hats towards the end of the Victorian era were enormous and wide-brimmed. They were covered with elaborate creations of silk flowers, feathers, ribbons, and sometimes even stuffed birds. Men also wore hats, they were called high hats. High hats were elegant and covered in silk or in beaver skin. They were tall in height and had a wide brim.

Video resource: BBC Learning Website – Art & Design (Textile): *Hats (A history of hats)*

The Victoria and Albert Museum website has a section on 19th century fashion (www.vam.ac.uk)

On the road: Traffic lights

Scratch is open source computer coding software available from MIT (www.scratch.mit.edu) In order to control the traffic light you will need a control box. This is a piece of hardware that has analogue and digital inputs (switches and sensors) and analogue and digital outputs (lights and motors). The control box is connected to the computer and needs associated software to control it. (Control software is either flowchart based, such as Flowol or Logicator, or iconic such as LEGO RoboLab or Junior Control Insight.)

Video resource: BBC Learning Website – Design Technology Video: *Circuits, batteries and power sources; Electrical circuits; Dangers of electricity, the adventures of electro mouse* and *Using circuits to make games and activities*

Year 6 Long-term planning

Design

The National Curriculum states that when designing and making, children should be taught to:
- use research and develop design criteria to inform the design of innovative, functional, appealing products that are fit for purpose, aimed at particular individuals or groups
- generate, develop, model and communicate their ideas through discussion, annotated sketches, cross-sectional and exploded diagrams, prototypes, pattern pieces and computer-aided design.

Research a range of areas to inform their designing and making process, including:
- famous entrepreneurs, food products from crops, garden bird tables, fairground rides, puppets, theatrical masks and headdresses, logos and branding.

Model and communicate their ideas through:
- drawings, illustrations, photographs and annotated diagrams
- using a standardised design sheet to convey their ideas
- mindmaps, spreadsheets and computer aided design
- using online design software and illustrated instructions.

Make

The National Curriculum states that when designing and making, children should be taught to:
- select from and use a wider range of tools and equipment to perform practical tasks (for example, cutting, shaping, joining and finishing), accurately
- select from and use a wider range of materials and components, including construction materials, textiles and ingredients, according to their functional properties and aesthetic qualities.

Use a range of tools across each area of design technology, including:
- utensils to cut and prepare food ingredients
- food processing equipment
- ICT design software
- scissors and card snips
- sewing equipment
- saw and PVA glue.

Use a range of materials to make their products, including:
- paper, card, cardboard and tissue paper
- wood strips and 10mm square wood
- newspaper, art straws and masking tape
- acrylic paints and varnish
- plain white t-shirts
- fabric materials and decorations
- simple electrical components including motors
- pulleys and gears.

Evaluate

The National Curriculum states that when designing and making, children should be taught to:
- investigate and analyse a range of existing products
- evaluate their ideas and products against their own design criteria and consider the views of others to improve their work
- understand how key events and individuals in design and technology have helped shape the world.

Investigate and evaluate a range of products including: bird tables, products made from strawberries and tomatoes, fairground rides, puppets, theatre masks and headdresses, logos and commercial brands.

Gain a better understanding of how design and technology have shaped the world through:
- researching entrepreneurs and writing business plans
- understanding how companies develop their brand.

Technical knowledge

The National Curriculum states that when designing and making, children should be taught to:
- apply their understanding of how to strengthen, stiffen and reinforce more complex structures
- understand and use mechanical systems in their products (for example, gears, pulleys, cams, levers and linkages)
- understand and use electrical systems in their products (for example, series circuits incorporating switches, bulbs, buzzers and motors)
- apply their understanding of computing to program, monitor and control their products.

Develop and consolidate technical knowledge in the following areas:
- mechanical systems involving gears and pulleys.
- strengthening and reinforcing complex structures.
- using electrical systems in products (switches, bulbs and motors).
- using computing to control their products.

Cooking and nutrition

The National Curriculum states that children should be taught to:
- understand and apply the principles of a healthy and varied diet
- prepare and cook a variety of predominantly savoury dishes using a range of cooking techniques
- understand seasonality, and know where and how ingredients are grown, reared, caught and processed.

Develop and consolidate their knowledge and understanding of healthy eating and nutrition by:
- preparing and cooking a range of foods that they have grown themselves
- understanding seasonality and how it affects ingredients that are grown.

Overview of progression in Year 6

Designing

Throughout units of work in Year 6 children:

- investigate similar products to get ideas, list key features and understand how they work
- describe the purpose of their products
- list design features that will appeal to intended users
- explain how parts and whole of products work and how it will be made
- research information about the needs and wants of users using surveys, interviews, questionnaires and web-based resources
- develop design criteria to inform ideas and develop a simple design specification as a guide
- use prototypes and pattern pieces
- use annotated sketches, cross-sectional drawings and exploded diagrams
- use computer aided design.

Making and technical knowledge: Cooking and nutrition

By designing and making food dishes from ingredients that they have grown, children:

- formulate step-by-step plans as a guide to making, producing lists of required tools, equipment and materials
- know that food is grown, reared, and caught in the UK, Europe and the wider world and that seasons may affect the food available
- know food is processed into ingredients that can be eaten or used in cooking
- know how to prepare and cook a variety of predominantly savoury dishes safely and hygienically including the use of a heat source
- know how to use a range of techniques, such as peeling, chopping, slicing, grating, mixing, spreading, kneading and baking
- measure food ingredients with increasing accuracy
- assemble ingredients to make recipes and apply a range of finishing techniques, with increasing accuracy.

Making and technical knowledge: Textiles

By designing and making a new puppet for a Punch and Judy show and a T-shirt to advertise a theatrical show, children:

- formulate step-by-step plans as a guide to making, producing lists of required tools, equipment and materials
- measure, mark out, cut and shape textile materials and components with increasing accuracy
- apply a range of finishing techniques, with increasing accuracy.

Year 6 Complete 'Overview of progression' is provided on the CD-ROM, including 'Making and technical knowledge: Construction', 'Making and technical knowledge: Sheet materials' and 'Evaluating' objectives.

◢SCHOLASTIC

Year 6 Medium-term planning: 1A In the garden:
From garden to table

Design brief: To design and make food dishes from ingredients which have been grown as an enterprise business.

P	Learning objectives	Creative, technical and practical activities
Designing	• To understand what enterprise means. • To create an action plan using pictures or a flow diagram. • To develop more than one design or adapt an initial design to produce a final design. • To use technical vocabulary when designing and planning to make a product.	This unit is designed to develop enterprise skills. Working in groups, children will learn about enterprise in a real format and experience producing something to sell. It encourages children to make money for a school project or charity. **Focused practical task (FPT)** This unit of work begins with children growing strawberries and tomatoes. **Evaluating existing products (EEP): Jams and chutneys** This forms part of a brainstorming session to develop ideas for what they could produce from their crops, for example, strawberry or blackberry jam or tomato chutney. These ideas can then be developed into a mindmap of enterprise ideas: • products to be made • costs in setting up the business/budget (inflows and outflows) • opportunities to sell their product • marketing their product (advertising/market research). From the mindmap children create an action plan to produce and market their product. (If possible, each group should be given a 'start-up grant'.) **Investigation** Children research how strawberries and tomatoes are grown in the UK and understand the seasonality of crops. (Visit a nearby farm, if possible.) They learn how these foods are grown overseas to enable them to be available all year round in the UK. They understand how this has brought new industries to developing regions of the world but how the transportation of such crops can affect the environment. Suggest children also research the business stories behind famous entrepreneurs.
Making	• To know that food is processed into ingredients for cooking. • To know that some foods are seasonal. • To prepare, join and combine ingredients accurately using a range of techniques. • To work safely and hygienically. • To prepare and cook food using a heat source.	During the making phase, children follow well-established recipes to create their products. All ingredients that they use should be costed and added to their budget sheet. Using information from their budget sheets, children need to decide on prices for their product in order to make a profit. (This should be carried out after they have made their product in order to assess how much product they have to sell.) Using a range of ICT applications, children design and make: • the appropriate packaging for their products • advertising (posters, advert for newsletters, flyers, radio jingle, short TV advert).
Evaluating	• To discuss the effectiveness of the method and techniques used in making the product. • To understand how individuals and companies in design technology have helped shape the world.	Throughout the project, each child or group should keep a budget spreadsheet that details expenditure and income. At the end of the project, part of the evaluation will be to record how much profit/loss was made. Children produce a report of their project including: • products they made (including the recipes) • how they marketed their product • profit/loss spreadsheet. **Extension**: Children understand that they have developed all the components of a business plan. They could then be challenged to create more ideas for enterprise projects and write the business plan before making the products.

Notes:

Strawberries and tomatoes are relatively easy to grow but children can also pick blackberries from the bushes when they are ripe for a free alternative. If it isn't possible to grow or pick these fruits, buy from a market or supermarket. Also, other fruits (or vegetables) can be used depending on what is in season.

Cross curricular links:

Mathematics: profits and loss, money

ICT: spreadsheets, multimedia presentations

English: persuasive writing, advertising

Year 6 Medium-term planning: 1B In the garden: Bird table

Design brief: To design and make a bird table to attract birds into the school garden.

P	Learning objectives	Creative, technical and practical activities
Designing	• To investigate similar products to get ideas and to use as a starting point for an original design. • To investigate similar products and list their key features. • To draw, photograph and label products to show an understanding of how they are made or how they work. • To develop more than one design or adapt an initial design to produce a final design. • To create plans that can be used by someone else to make the product.	In this unit of work, children are creating a prototype model of a bird table. They will then present their prototype model to the class in the form of a 'dragons den' presentation. **Evaluating existing products (EEP): Bird tables** From a PowerPoint presentation showing different bird tables, discuss what makes a good bird table. From a range of photographs, select five bird tables and display on a sheet of paper and label and annotate pictures to show key features of a good bird table. List three features of a good bird table which will be the design criteria by which the finished product will be judged against, such as: • box for nesting • area for feeding • covered area for shelter • area for bathing. The 'My design sheet' could be used for this purpose. **Focused practical task (FPT): Strengthening sheet materials** Allow children to undertake investigation into how to strengthen thin card through folding, zig zag, creating tubes and triangles. Demonstrate how corrugated cardboard is made. **Designing** Teach children how to draw 3D shapes and then to incorporate this skill into their designs. Children draw a design for a bird table, labelling and annotating the 'three key features'. This forms their design sheet. They also list the materials and tools that will be needed to construct the bird table. They write instructions for how to assemble the bird table from the sheet materials.
Making	• To choose appropriate sheet materials that are fit for purpose. • To create a frame structure with diagonal struts for added strength. • To cut accurately and safely following lines and markings. • To draw and create nets of 3D shapes. • To join and combine materials using glue to fix them together. • To apply a range of decorative finishing techniques.	From their design sheet, children construct their prototype bird table from thick card and cardboard. They also use other materials to complete their bird table. Key teaching points for working with sheet materials: • creating 3D shapes from nets • strengthening 3D shapes and sheet materials using wooden frames and/or diagonal struts • strengthening sheet material methods, for example, tubes for upright structures • joining two structures/sheet materials together by gluing or using masking tape. Once the structure is complete it should be painted brown to give a wooden effect.
Evaluating	• To list the ways in which the finished product meets the design criteria. • To discuss the effectiveness of the method and techniques used in making the product.	Children take a photograph of their finished prototype. This is enlarged and annotated for their 'dragons den' presentation. They may also want to provide photographic evidence of the design and making phases, as part of their presentation. During the presentation they may want to focus on: • how the bird table meets the original design criteria • the methods they have used to strengthen their structure.

Notes:
If facilities exist, this unit of work can be adapted to allow the prototype to be constructed out of wood.
Extend the activity by using the step-by-step instructions to make a 'Bird table alarm', available on the Scholastic web site (www.scholastic.co.uk/100designandtechnology).

Cross-curricular links:
PSHE: improving the local environment

Year 6 Medium-term planning: 2A At the fair: Fairground ride

Design brief: To design and make a model of a fairground ride.

P	Learning objectives	Creative, technical and practical activities
Designing	• To use labelled drawings and notes to explain how their product will be made. • To use labelled drawings and notes to explain how their product will work. • To use technical vocabulary when designing and planning to make a product.	**Evaluating existing products (EEP): Fairground rides** Show a selection of images and/or video clips of fairground rides and discuss rides children may have been on at a fairground. Ask children to explain: • how the rides move (rotational or linear or other) • the speed of the rides. **Technical knowledge** Construction kits: through experimenting with a range of pulleys, drive belts and gears children understand: • how the size of the pulleys and gears affects the speed of rotation • how pulleys and gears can change the direction of rotation. Working in small groups, provide children with a simple electrical circuit including a switch, motor, pulleys, elastic band (drive belt) and thick cardboard to act as a base. They need to construct a motor system to drive a rotational fairground ride. There are a number of features to consider: • The rotating part of the product turns on an axle which must be supported by a strong framework for the ride to remain stable. • The drive belt (elastic band) must be at the right tension – tight enough to turn the mechanism but not too tight to de-stable the mechanism. • A small pulley on the motor and a large one attached to the ride will considerably decrease the speed of rotation. Children have now made the motor section of their fairground ride. Explain that their ride can either be horizontal (carousel) or vertical (Ferris wheel). **Designing** When designing their fairground ride, children need to consider: • the motor, drive system and electrical circuit • making a stable frame for the motor (cardboard or wood frame) • the rotating part of the ride (explain that this part of the model will be made using art straws) • the 'cars' that will hold the passengers on the ride – will they be fixed or will they have a moving joint?
Making	• To use a simple circuit in a model with switches, bulbs and motors. • To create a frame structure with diagonal struts for added strength. • To create stable frames using a range of materials. • To accurately cut wood using a range of tools accurately. • To control a model using an ICT control program.	Children make the rotating part of the ride first from art straws and card. They need to consider how they will join the straws and also how they will strengthen the structure by using diagonal struts. Once this structure has been completed it can then be decorated. Children then make the cars, decorate them and attach to the ride structure. The rotating structure should be tested to make sure it rotates freely. Next children create the rigid structure to hold the motor and drive mechanism. They can use cardboard or make a wooden frame using a 10mm square piece of wood. The drive mechanism is then fitted to the rigid structure and then the rotating structure is fixed to the drive. The model is complete but can be enhanced by: • adding additional decoration/working lights • using computer software to control the model.
Evaluating	• To list the ways in which the finished product meets the design criteria. • To discuss the effectiveness of the method and techniques used in making the product.	**Evaluating their own ideas and products** • How good does the model look? • Is it decorated well? • Does the model rotate freely without the motor? • Does the motor drive the model at an appropriate speed? • Is the framework for holding the model strong and stable? Give the children copies of the 'Product evaluation sheet' from the CD-ROM to write up their evaluations.

Notes:
A display of all the rides, with their design sheets, will make an impressive class/school display.

Cross-curricular links:
Science: pulleys in physics

Year 6 Medium-term planning: 2B At the fair: Punch and Judy puppet

Design brief: To design and make a new character puppet for a Punch and Judy show.

P	Learning objectives	Creative, technical and practical activities
Designing	• To investigate similar products to get ideas and to use as a starting point for an original design. • To plan a sequence of actions to make a product. • To use labelled drawings and notes to explain how their product will be made. • To create an action plan using pictures or a flow diagram. • To create plans that can be used by someone else to make the product.	**Evaluating existing products (EPP)** While conducting research into Punch and Judy shows: • view video clips of performances • identify the main characters • download and display pictures of the puppets identifying the key features and display on A3 sheet. Decide on a new character. *What are the key features that will immediately identify this character?* (facial features, colour of costume and additional features) **Designing** Children design the puppet in two phases (they draw annotated design sheets with labels): 1. Head – what it will be made of (papier mache/mod roc/wooden spoon) Hair – style and how it will be made /materials Hat – style, materials and colour 2. Body – what it will be made of (stem of the spoon + wooden arms in a shape of a cross) Fabrics to make the costume Decorations Children should identify and write an action plan (with diagrams where necessary). Children follow each other's plans to construct the puppet. They should elaborate on the following: 1. Create body shape using wooden spoon and dowelling to form cross – secure with modelling wire. 2. Create basic head shape on wooden spoon with newspaper. Cover and mould details using plasticised bandages (mod roc). 3. Paint and add further details to the sculptured head (facial details, woollen hair). 4. Create puppet costume (body and hat) to fit over the body armature by making a fabric pattern and include details of the decoration on the costume.
Making	• To create stable frames using a range of materials. • To accurately cut wood using a range of tools. • To join fabrics together using a range of different sewing techniques and/or fastenings. • To cut a range of fabrics accurately using a pattern. • To apply a range of decorative techniques to different fabric materials.	In making the puppet, children follow their action plan in order. However, they should plan their work so that they can complete other tasks whilst certain elements, like the mod-roc head, are drying. During the making, children take a number of photographs of the stages of the puppet construction, particularly focusing on the skills and techniques being used. Children should make the puppet armature first; this will allow them to measure the finished armature as a guide to creating the puppet costume. When making the costume, suggest that children draw a paper pattern to attach to the fabric with pins as a guide before cutting out using scissors. The costume pieces are joined using a running stitch (leaving a seam allowance) before decorations are added using fabric pens, glitter, beads, sequins, etc.
Evaluating	• To consider and list ways in which their design or product could be improved. • To discuss the effectiveness of the materials, the method and techniques used in making the product.	The evaluation process involves the children referring back to their original action plan, discussing with a partner and amending the plan to take into account their practical experience of making the puppet. Using word processing and the photographs taken during the making process, they create a brochure that gives clear illustrated instructions on how to make a puppet for a Punch and Judy show. They also include a list of the materials and tools that are needed.

Cross-curricular links:
Drama/English: writing a new play script for a Punch and Judy show incorporating the newly designed puppet.

Year 6 Medium-term planning: 3A Down the catwalk: Theatrical mask

Design brief: To design and make a mask or a headpiece for a theatrical performance.

P	Learning objectives	Creative, technical and practical activities
Designing phase	• To investigate similar products to get ideas and to use as a starting point for an original design. • To use labelled drawings and notes to explain how their product will be made. • To use technical vocabulary when designing and planning to make a product.	**Evaluating existing products (EEP): Masks** Collect images and examples of carnival masks and African masks to make a visual resource to inspire the children. Discuss the key design features: • What are the key design factors of the mask/headdress that are needed for the actors? • What are the other design factors that will make a good mask/headdress? **Generating, developing, modelling and communicating ideas** Show children the original animated film of *The Lion King*. Show images of costumes from *The Lion King* musical and identify differences between a mask and a headdress. Each child chooses a character from the film and researches and collects photographs and images of their chosen character. **Focused practical task (FPT)** Show children how to make newspaper rods and investigate the best methods of joining these rods to make the frame for a headdress. Working in pairs, children make a basic headdress that fits their partner. **Designing** Children decide whether to create a mask or headdress. They then draw a design for it and through diagrams, labels and annotations, show clearly how it will be made, the materials that will be used and the methods of joining the pieces together. This will act as their guide for the making process.
Making	• To choose appropriate sheet materials that are fit for purpose. • To join and combine materials using glue to fix them together. • To apply a range of decorative finishing techniques. • To create stable frames using a range of materials.	**Making the mask** Suggested ways of making the mask. • Use thick card or corrugated cardboard that is cut into the desired shape. This shape is then covered with layers of coloured tissue paper and watered-down PVA glue (equal amounts of water and PVA). When this dries, this will provide a sturdy and colourful mask shape. • Use plastic white face masks – which are available from educational suppliers – and cut down to the desired shape and cover with tissue paper and PVA glue. Newspaper rods can be added to the mask to enlarge it. **Making the headdress** • Children use the basic headdresses made in the FPT session and then add additional newspaper rods to create the basic framework. This is then covered with layers of tissue paper and watered down PVA glue. **Decoration** Children use a range of materials and decorative techniques to complete the mask (paint, glitter, tissue paper, feathers etc.).
Evaluating	• To consider and list ways in which their design or product could be improved. • To list the ways in which the finished product meets the design criteria.	**Evaluating their own ideas and products** Give the children copies of the 'Product evaluation sheet' from the CD-ROM to write up their evaluations. Children self-evaluate their mask or headdress against the key design features (see background knowledge). They mark against each design feature (marks out of ten) and then justify each score – verbally or in writing. For the two features that they gave the lowest marks to, they suggest ways in which the product could be improved. As part of the evaluation, children host a fashion show of their headdresses and masks and parade their designs down the catwalk.

Notes:
This unit of work is based on the musical *The Lion King*, however, it can adapted for any theatrical show, particularly one in which the children are actually performing. The focus on mask-making can also be altered or extended to include elements of costume design. A selection of mask templates can be found on the Scholastic web site (www.scholastic.co.uk/100designandtechnology).

Cross-curricular links:
Drama/English: *The Lion King*
Art and design: mask making

Year 6 Medium-term planning: 3B Down the catwalk: T-shirt

Design brief: To design and make a T-shirt to advertise a theatrical show.

P	Learning objectives	Creative, technical and practical activities
Designing	• To understand that logos and badges help to establish an identity. • To draw, photograph and label products to show an understanding of how they are made or how they work. • To develop more than one design or adapt an initial design to produce a final design. • To use a computer to help in designing or modelling ideas.	**Generating, developing, modelling and communicating ideas** **Discuss**: *What is meant by a logo?* Facilitate a quiz on famous logos – can children identify the brands? In groups, children research and produce their own logo quiz. **Evaluating existing products (EEP): Logos** Provide children with well-known logos. *What are the features of a good logo?* Children create a logo of their own using ICT, for example, use www.cooltext.com. Show a PowerPoint presentation of famous theatrical/musical show logos and ask children to annotate examples identifying key features. **Designing** Children design a new theatrical logo for a show opening in a local theatre. This can either be a free choice or linked to shows/films based on animals, for example, *Cats*, *The Lion King* or *The Jungle Book*: Children should be encouraged to make some initial sketches of ideas and then produce a number of possible designs for the logo. They discuss their designs with other 'class designers' before developing one of them into the final design. The final design is created by hand or produced using ICT design software. (Hand-drawn designs can be scanned and a digital copy made for future use.) In addition, there are a number of online websites for designing T-shirts that children can use.
Making	• To apply a range of decorative techniques to different fabric materials.	The design should be transferred onto iron-transfer paper using an inkjet or laser printer. Then, with the help of an adult, carefully ironed onto a plain white T-shirt. **Developing merchandise** Children research websites of current London theatrical shows or merchandise shops to find out what other kinds of products are sold as well as T-shirts. They understand that once a logo has been created it can be applied to a range of products. Give children, in groups, the opportunity to create a range of merchandise projects based on their logo design: • badge (if the school has a badge maker) • mug (water transfer using decal paper) • bookmark or bag • calendar (can be created from Microsoft Publisher template) • poster advertising the show at a local theatre • CD/DVD cover. Children can create a display of the merchandise projects they have created. **Extension** (link with ICT): Children create a website page to advertise/sell their theatre merchandise.
Evaluating	• To express a preference about the likes and dislikes of their finished product. • To understand how individuals and companies in design technology have helped shape the world.	**Evaluating their own ideas and products** The merchandising items and ideas are priced by the designer and added to a whole-class display. Each member of the class is given a certain amount of 'pretend money' to spend on merchandise projects (apart from their own). They are encouraged to buy the merchandise that is most appealing and has a quality finish. Products are judged by the amount of money generated. **Extension**: Children can complete the online learning module about how a high street store (Marks and Spencer) has developed its brand and image since the late 19th century. http://www.mylearning.org/the-mands-company-archive/birth-of-a-brand/

Notes:
Although this unit of work is based around a theatrical show, it can easily be adapted for any company, local visitor attraction or new school logo, etc.

Cross-curricular links:
English: persuasive writing, advertising
ICT: desktop publishing, computer-aided design

Year 6 Background knowledge

In the garden: From garden to table

Enterprise is all about making things happen. It is about having the skills and abilities to turn creative ideas into business success. People who are famous entrepreneurs that the children might know include: Lord Alan Sugar, Victoria Beckham, Richard Branson and Levi Roots.

There are various simple recipes for making chutney and jam

For chutney, the main ingredients to add to the tomatoes are: onions, butter, white wine vinegar, Demerara sugar.

For jam, the main ingredients to add to the strawberries are: caster sugar, lemon juice, butter.

In the garden: Bird table

Scholastic online: Make a Bird Table Alarm activity could extend this unit of work further (www.scholastic.co.uk/100designandtechnology)

At the fair: Fairground ride

www.technologytom.com has an extensive range of ideas for design technology, including fairground rides.

At the fair: Punch and Judy puppet

Video resource: BBC Learning Website – Design Technology Video: *Putting on a puppet show (parts 1 and 2)*

Down the catwalk: Theatrical mask

Key design factors of the mask/headpiece:

- sturdy and comfortable to wear
- good visibility for the actor
- allows the actor to speak and sing clearly
- clearly reflect the character being portrayed
- bright, colourful
- visually exciting with the animal features over-exaggerated.

One of the main considerations that children should be aware of when making their masks is to balance the need for strength and a sturdy design against the weight of the mask – light materials such as newspaper and tissue paper should be used.

There is an excellent website for the UK production of *The Lion King* with a range of resources for primary schools.

Video resource: BBC Learning Website – Design Technology Video: *Making masks*

Down the catwalk: T-shirt

Transfer paper for the T-shirt logo is widely available. The type of transfer paper needed depends on whether an inkjet or laser printer is being used to print the design.

Video resource: BBC Learning Website – Design Technology Video: *Designing a logo*

On-line websites for creating T-shirts:
www.customlink.com
www.opentshirts.com

Websites for theatre merchandise:
www.dresscircle.com
www.theatre-shop.com

Progression in design & technology at Key Stage 1

Children should have the opportunity to:
- Use creativity and imagination to design and make products that solve real and relevant problems and to share and clarify ideas through discussion.
- Work confidently within a range of contexts, such as imaginary, story-based, home, school, garden, playground, local community, industry and the wider environment.
- Consider their own and others' needs, wants and values when designing and making products.
- Acquire a broad range of subject knowledge and use learning from disciplines such as mathematics, science, computing and art.
- Learn how to take risks, becoming resourceful, innovative, enterprising and capable citizens.
- Develop a critical understanding of design and technology and its impact on daily life and the wider world through evaluation of past and present design and technology.
- Understand the essential contribution high-quality design and technology education makes to the creativity, culture, wealth and well-being of the nation.

Designing	Making and technical knowledge: Cooking and nutrition	Making and technical knowledge: Textiles
Understand contexts, users and purposes: • Consider similar products to get ideas. • State what products they are designing and making. • Say whether their products are for themselves or other users. • Describe what their products are for. • Say how their products will work. • Say how they will make their products suitable for their intended users. • Use simple design criteria to help develop their ideas. Generate, develop, model and communicate ideas: • Generate ideas from their own experiences. • Use knowledge of existing products to help form ideas. • Develop and communicate ideas by talking and drawing. • Model ideas by exploring materials, components and construction kits and by making templates and mock-ups. Use information and communication technology, where appropriate, to develop and communicate their ideas.	Planning: • Plan by suggesting what to do next. • Select from a range of tools and equipment, explaining their choices. • Select from a range of materials and components according to their characteristics. Where food comes from: • Know that all food comes from plants or animals. • Know that food has to be farmed, grown elsewhere (e.g. home) or caught. Food preparation, cooking and nutrition: • Name and sort foods into the five groups. • Know that everyone should eat at least five portions of fruit and vegetables every day. • Follow procedures for safety and hygiene. • Use a range of food ingredients. • Measure and weigh ingredients. • Prepare and assemble ingredients. • Prepare simple dishes safely and hygienically, without using a heat source. • Use techniques such as cutting, peeling and grating. **Technical knowledge** • Know about the simple working characteristics of materials and components. • Know that food ingredients should be combined according to their sensory characteristics. • Use the correct technical vocabulary to describe food and ingredients, including taste, smell, texture, feel.	Planning: • Plan by suggesting what to do next. • Select from a range of tools and equipment, explaining their choices. • Select from a range of materials and components according to their characteristics. Practical skills and techniques: • Follow procedures for safety and hygiene. • Use a range of materials and components, including textiles. • Measure, mark out, cut and shape materials and components. • Assemble, join and combine materials and components. • Use finishing techniques, including those from art and design. **Technical knowledge** • Know about the simple working characteristics of materials and components. • Know that a 3D textile product can be assembled from two identical fabric shapes. • Use the correct technical vocabulary to describe sewing and joining fabrics and decorations.

Progression in design & technology at Key Stage 1, continued

Children should have the opportunity to:
- Use creativity and imagination to design and make products that solve real and relevant problems and to share and clarify ideas through discussion.
- Work confidently within a range of contexts, such as imaginary, story-based, home, school, garden, playground, local community, industry and the wider environment.
- Consider their own and others' needs, wants and values when designing and making products.
- Acquire a broad range of subject knowledge and use learning from disciplines such as mathematics, science, computing and art.
- Learn how to take risks, becoming resourceful, innovative, enterprising and capable citizens.
- Develop a critical understanding of design and technology and its impact on daily life and the wider world through evaluation of past and present design and technology.
- Understand the essential contribution high-quality design and technology education makes to the creativity, culture, wealth and well-being of the nation.

Making and technical knowledge: Construction	Making and technical knowledge: Sheet materials	Evaluating
Planning: • Plan by suggesting what to do next. • Select from a range of tools and equipment, explaining their choices. • Select from a range of materials and components according to their characteristics. Practical skills and techniques: • Follow procedures for safety and hygiene. • Use a range of materials and components, including construction materials and kits, and mechanical components. • Measure, mark out, cut and shape materials and components. • Assemble, join and combine materials and components. • Use finishing techniques, including those from art and design. **Technical knowledge** • Know about the simple working characteristics of materials and components. • Know about the movement of simple mechanisms such as levers, sliders, wheels and axles. • Use the correct technical vocabulary to describe mechanical processes, including wheels and axles.	Planning: • Plan by suggesting what to do next. • Select from a range of tools and equipment, explaining their choices. • Select from a range of materials and components according to their characteristics. Practical skills and techniques: • Follow procedures for safety and hygiene. • Use a range of materials and components, including construction materials and kits. • Measure, mark out, cut and shape materials and components. • Assemble, join and combine materials and components. • Use finishing techniques, including those from art and design. **Technical knowledge** • Know about the simple working characteristics of materials and components. • Know how freestanding structures can be made stronger, stiffer and more stable. • Use the correct technical vocabulary for different sheet materials, including joining and strengthening.	Own ideas and products: • Talk about design ideas and what they are making. • Make simple judgements about their products and ideas against design criteria. • Suggest how their products could be improved. • Express likes and dislikes of finished products. Existing products – explore: • what products are • who products are for • what products are for • how products work • how products are used • where products might be used • what materials products are made from • what they like and dislike about products.

Progression in design & technology at Key Stage 2

Children should have the opportunity to:
- Use creativity and imagination to design and make products that solve real and relevant problems and to share and clarify ideas through discussion.
- Work confidently within a range of contexts, such as imaginary, story-based, home, school, garden, playground, local community, industry and the wider environment.
- Consider their own and others' needs, wants and values when designing and making products.
- Acquire a broad range of subject knowledge and use learning from disciplines such as mathematics, science, computing and art.
- Learn how to take risks, becoming resourceful, innovative, enterprising and capable citizens.
- Develop a critical understanding of design and technology and its impact on daily life and the wider world through evaluation of past and present design and technology.
- Understand the essential contribution high-quality design and technology education makes to the creativity, culture, wealth and well-being of the nation.

Designing	Making and technical knowledge: Cooking and nutrition	Making and technical knowledge: Textiles
To understand contexts, users and purposes: • Investigate similar products to get ideas, list key features and understand how they work. • Describe the purpose of their products. • List design features that will appeal to intended users. • Explain how parts and whole of products work and how it will be made. • Research information about the needs and wants of users; *upper* using surveys, interviews, questionnaires and web-based resources. • Develop design criteria to inform ideas; *upper* developing a simple design specification as a guide. To generate, develop, model and communicate ideas: • Use prototypes and pattern pieces. • Use annotated sketches, cross-sectional drawings and exploded diagrams. • Use computer-aided design. Make design decisions taking account of the availability of resources; later taking account of constraints such as time, resources and cost.	Planning: • Selecting and explaining choice of: tools and equipment; materials and components. • List the order of the main stages of making; *upper* produce lists of tools, equipment and materials. • *Upper*: Formulate step-by-step plans as a guide to making. Where food comes from: • Know that food is grown, reared, and caught in the UK, Europe and the wider world; *upper* that seasons may affect food. • *Upper*: Understand how food is processed into ingredients that can be eaten or used in cooking. Food preparation, cooking and nutrition: • Know how to prepare and cook a variety of predominantly savoury dishes safely and hygienically including a heat source. • Know how to use a range of techniques: peeling, chopping, slicing, grating, mixing, spreading, kneading and baking. • Measure, assemble ingredients and apply finishing techniques, with increasing accuracy. • Know that a healthy diet is made up from a variety and balance of different food and drink; *upper* that to be active and healthy, food and drink are needed to provide energy for the body. • *Upper*: Understand that recipes can be adapted, that ingredients can be fresh, pre-cooked and processed; later that a recipe can be adapted by adding or substituting one or more ingredients.	Planning: • Select suitable tools/equipment, materials/components. • Explain choice of tools and equipment depending on skills and techniques to be used. • Explain choice of materials, components to fit functional properties and aesthetic qualities. • List/order the main stages of making; *upper* produce lists of tools, equipment and materials. • *Upper*: Formulate step-by-step plans as a guide to making. Practical skills and techniques: • Follow procedures for safety and hygiene. • Measure, mark out, cut, shape textile materials/components with increasing accuracy. • Assemble, join and combine materials and components, apply a range of finishing techniques with increasing accuracy. • *Upper*: Use techniques that involve a number of steps, demonstrate resourcefulness with practical problems. **Technical knowledge** • Understand functional and aesthetic qualities of materials and that materials can be combined and mixed to create more useful characteristics. • Use an increasing and correct technical vocabulary. • Know that a single fabric shape can be used to make a 3D textiles product; *upper* that a 3D textiles product can be made from a combination of fabric shapes.

Progression in design & technology at Key Stage 2, continued

Making and technical knowledge: Construction	Making and technical knowledge: Sheet materials	Evaluating
Planning: • Select suitable tools/equipment, materials/components. • Explain choice of tools and equipment depending on skills and techniques to be used. • Explain choice of materials and components to fit functional properties and aesthetic qualities. • List/order the main stages of making; *upper* produce lists of tools, equipment and materials. • *Upper*: Formulate step-by-step plans as a guide to making. Practical skills and techniques: • Follow procedures for safety and hygiene. • Measure, mark out, cut, shape materials/components with increasing accuracy. • Assemble, join and combine materials and components, apply a range of finishing techniques with increasing accuracy. • *Upper*: Use techniques that involve a number of steps. • *Upper*: Demonstrate resourcefulness when tackling practical problems. **Technical knowledge** • Understand functional and aesthetic qualities of materials. • Understand that materials can be combined and mixed to create more useful characteristics. • Use an increasing and correct technical vocabulary to describe different mechanisms – mechanical and electrical. • Understand that mechanical and electrical systems have an input, process and output. • Understand mechanical systems: levers and linkages or pneumatic systems create movement; *upper* cams or pulleys or gears. • Understand how simple electrical circuits and components can be used to create functional products; *upper* more complex electrical circuits and components. • Know how to program a computer to control their products; *upper* monitor environmental changes and control their products.	Planning: • Select suitable tools and equipment, materials and components. • Explain choice of tools and equipment depending on skills and techniques to be used. • Explain choice of materials and components to fit functional properties and aesthetic qualities. • List the order of the main stages of making; *upper* produce lists of required tools, equipment and materials. • *Upper*: Formulate step-by-step plans as a guide to making. Practical skills and techniques: • Follow procedures for safety and hygiene. • Measure, mark out, cut and shape sheet materials and components with increasing accuracy. • Assemble, join and combine materials and components with increasing accuracy. • Apply a range of finishing techniques, with increasing accuracy. • *Upper*: Use techniques that involve a number of steps. • *Upper*: Demonstrate resourcefulness when tackling practical problems. **Technical knowledge** • Use learning from science and mathematics. • Understand functional and aesthetic qualities of materials. • Understand that materials can be combined and mixed to create more useful characteristics. • Use an increasing and correct technical vocabulary to describe methods of strengthening and joining different sheet materials. • Know how to make strong, stiff shell structures; *upper* how to reinforce and strengthen a 3D framework.	Own ideas and products: • Express likes and dislikes of finished products. • Identify strengths and areas for development in ideas and products. • Consider and list ways to improve designs or products, taking into account the views of others, e.g. intended users. • Refer to design criteria during progress and to evaluate completed products. • *Upper*: Critically evaluate products – the quality of design, effectiveness of materials used, method of manufacture and fitness for purpose. • *Upper*: Evaluate ideas and products against original design specification. Existing products – investigate and analyse: • design of products • manufacture of products • chosen materials • methods of construction used • effectiveness of products • fitness for purpose • effectiveness of meeting user needs and wants • *Lower*: designer and maker of products • where and when products designed and made • whether products can be recycled or reused • *Upper*: how much products cost to make • how innovate products are • how sustainable materials used are • what impact products have beyond their intended purpose. Key events and individuals: • Know about inventors, designers, engineers, chefs and manufacturers who have developed ground-breaking products.

Progression grid adapted from Design and Technology Progression Framework (DATA, 2014)

SCHOLASTIC

Essential support for the 2014 National Curriculum

Fully in line with the new curriculum objectives

Plan with confidence with 100 Lessons Planning Guides

Complete planning frameworks with long and medium-term guidance for Years 1-6

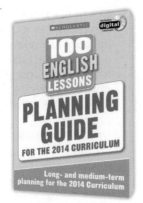

9781407128399

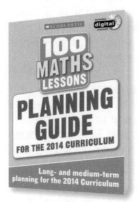

9781407128405

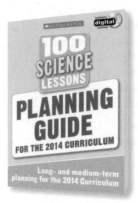

9781407128412

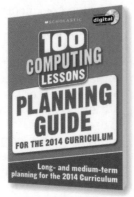

9781407128610

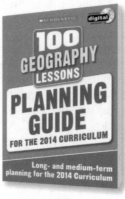

9781407128597

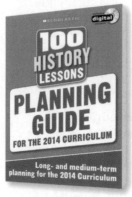

9781407128603

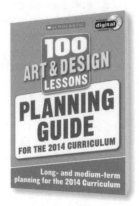

9781407140865

9781407140858

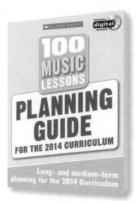

9781407140841

Order at www.scholastic.co.uk/100lessons **or call us on** 0845 603 9091